MELVIN W. DONAHO is Professor of
Communications and JOHN L. MEYER is
Associate Professor of Speech
Communications. Both are at the State
University of New York, Plattsburgh.

MELVIN W. DONAHO
AND
JOHN L. MEYER

HOW TO GET THE JOB YOU WANT

A Guide to Résumés, Interviews, and Job- Hunting Strategy

Prentice Hall Press • New York

Library of Congress Cataloging-in-Publication Data

Donaho, Melvin W.
  How to get the job you want.

   Bibliography: p.
   Includes index.
   1. Applications for positions.   2. Résumés
(Employment)   3. Employment interviewing.   I. Meyer,
John L., joint author.   II. Title.
   HF5383.D57   650'.14   76-19005
   ISBN 0–13–407254–5
   ISBN 0–13–407247–2 pbk.

Published in 1986 by Prentice Hall Press
A Division of Simon & Schuster, Inc.
Gulf + Western Building
One Gulf + Western Plaza
New York, NY 10023

Originally published by Prentice-Hall, Inc.

PRENTICE HALL PRESS is a trademark of Simon & Schuster, Inc.

Manufactured in the United States of America

10   9   8   7   6   5   4   3   2

Contents

Prefatory Letter

September, 1976

Dear Reader:

Being out of a job can be both frustrating and frightening. Similarly, the transition between careers can be a trying time filled with adjustment, anxiety, and anguish. During periods of rapid changes in the job market and especially during periods of high unemployment, we talk frequently with such disappointed and despairing persons. Some say that they simply cannot find jobs. Others complain that they cannot land jobs once they have found them. Occasionally, however, we meet persons who are thrilled to find their expectations realized and to see that their career plans have "paid-off."

There is a difference between merely accepting a job that "just happens along" and carefully designing a career leading to a professionally enhancing position. The former is just luck, a happy accident; the latter may also include good fortune, but it is combined with thoughtful planning and preparation.

What can you expect from reading what is within? This book presents ideas for finding and landing a position. Specifically, the content centers on the careful preparation of letters of application, the writing of professional *résumés,* and the preparation, and follow-up stages of the employment interview. You may be assured that it is a professional guide designed to help you to help yourself without spending several hundreds of dollars in fees.

We sincerely hope that you will find something of value in each of the chapters. We have purposely designed checklists and aids for all readers, whether the reader is writing a letter of job application, organizing a *résumé,* or preparing for the next employment interview.

We cannot guarantee that reading this book will get you a job or a new position. We are certain that it will answer many of your employment-seeking questions; it will give you valuable ideas and suggestions; it will provide directions to a professional approach to the problem. If you study this book carefully and follow its suggestions and overall approach—an approach which requires both competence and commitment—you will develop greater confidence in yourself and in your chances for success.

We wish you much success as you change careers.

Sincerely yours,

MELVIN W. DONAHO

JOHN L. MEYER

Introduction

"Where can I find a job? How do you locate a new position?" These two questions are frequently expressed in desperation. They often seem unanswerable, even for those who have had years of experience in high executive positions.

However, you may already have the answers to these urgent questions. Reflect for a minute! How did you get your first job? Can you remember when you were a youngster and took your first paid job? Chances are it was acquired by word of mouth. Perhaps your parents or a friend told you about a vacancy. Perhaps, if you were fortunate, reports of your capability, ability, or reliability came to the attention of an employer who asked your parents about your availability. You were fortunate indeed if someone requested your services.

The *word of mouth approach* often depends upon your *visibility* and *availability*. You may be wise to find where the jobs are (if they exist) or where they may be in the future. Then let the employers of those positions know that you are ready, willing, and able to fill them.

To find a job or locate a vacant position, you should begin by making contacts. Your visibility and availability must be with people who can either make employment decisions or influence those who do. You should contact your former employers. They may have new openings or they may have recently received resignations. Contacts can be made at union meetings, conferences, or through professional organizations. Job recruiters are often available at high school and college career nights.

Don't hibernate with the problem of joblessness. Get out and meet people. If you are living in the area where you'd like a job, meet with people at social gatherings and at church meetings. Meet them while doing volunteer work or at campaign headquarters. Talk to people about employment opportunities and new developments in your field. Seek out people who are employed in your profession and inquire about employment possibilities.

If you are out of a job, you are likely to feel hopeless or left out. You may, understandably, feel desperate—with no place to turn. Ironically, such feelings of frustration and despair are also felt by the person who has a job but is unhappy with it or feels it is pointless. Rather than feeling left out, the person in the wrong job is likely to feel boxed in. The frustrations for both are similar.

The answer lies in opening doors to job opportunities. Mr. or Ms. Jobless can no more afford to shut themselves out than Mr. or Ms. Job-full can afford to shut themselves in. What are the doors to job opportunities? Again, let's reflect on how jobs are acquired by ourselves and by those around us.

1. One of the first doors to turn to is "job advertisements". Whether you find them in the *New York Times,* the local newspaper, trade magazines, or professional journals, job advertisements are a quick guide to finding what types of work are available, where the jobs are located, and often, what wages are being paid. Affirmative action plans (which are positive procedures of firms for hiring minority employees) require companies to advertise widely. As "equal opportunity employers" (required by federal and state governments), organizations are now advertising positions more widely and in more and different publications then ever before. Some commercial radio stations have employment announcements. Bulletin boards from shopping centers to personnel offices are likely to contain ads for "help wanted." Educational television stations occasionally broadcast an "employment bulletin board." State and federal positions ranging from janitors to high level managers are advertised in state and federal offices and buildings. Often these advertisements contain or are appended to job descriptions.

These job descriptions (often influenced by affirmative action requirements) spell out such criteria as skills necessary, experience required, and deadlines for the receipt of applications. Such important details can help to guide you in determining whether these are potential jobs for you.

2. Another source of job opportunities is found behind the doors of vocational guidance counselors and personnel offices. If you are presently connected with an organization (college or firm) you may discover that the counselor or personnel manager comes into contact with tips on job vacancies. This is often the contact point for job recruiters who visit the organization. Vocational counselors can often help to arrange meetings for you with job recruiters. Counselors frequently have access to the most recent job availability lists. Some counseling offices have microfilm or microfiche vacancy notices for jobs across the country and abroad. These offices are often in touch with several job dissemination services.

3. A third door which can open job opportunities to you is that of public employment agencies and placement services. State-operated employment agencies (currently close to 2,000 offices in 50 states in conjunction with the U.S. Employment Service of the Department of Labor) will, with no cost to you, provide information regarding jobs within the state for which you are qualified. They, too, will help to make contacts with recruiters or actual employers for you. Often they will arrange for aptitude tests, vocational counseling, and actual job interviews in the state office itself.

For a small fee to cover the administrative costs, placement services connected with your professional organizations will also serve as a go-between between employer and employee. You may want to contact your professional organization or attend one of its conventions to inquire about their placement service. They can often provide you with lists of job vacancies from employers as well as providing those employers with your credentials.

4. Private employment agencies (in addition to public city, state, and federal agencies) abound in almost every large city in the country. Often they will guarantee to find you a job or

you pay them nothing. One source warns, however, that such agency fees run from five to fifteen percent of the annual starting salary. Where not regulated by state law, such fees may run as high as twenty to thirty per cent. You should, therefore, "know exactly what the financial arrangement is."[1]

In some instances, however, it may be financially sound to engage the services of an expensive private agency. If you don't have a pay check coming in, if you are accustomed to a moderately high income, or if you can't afford to spend six months time in searching for a really good job, it may be wise to rely on the speedy services and guarantees of such an agency. It should also be noted that some large companies work through such private employment agencies, or employment consultants, to make sure that they receive only highly qualified and well-suited candidates. The consultants, who may administer personality and psychological screening tests as a partial basis for their recommendations to the employer, may be paid by the firm. Some of these agencies operate on a fee-paid basis. This means that the employer pays the entire fee to the agency. Occasionally the employee pays the agency fee and after a trial period of satisfactory employment is reimbursed, either totally or partially, by the company.

The admonition, made earlier, is perhaps a wise consumer tip—"Know what the financial arrangement is." To such advice we might add, "Know the type of agency with which you are dealing." For today there are employment agencies and consultant firms that work exclusively for certain industries or fields (e.g., engineers or public accountants). If you should want to know about such agencies in your particular field, get a copy of the directory which lists such agencies by specialty. One is entitled *Employment Directions 1975.*[2]

The several doors to employment opportunities explained so far—job advertisements, vocational guidance counselors,

[1]"Some Professional Tips on How to Find a Job," *Better Homes and Gardens,* 53, no. 4, (1975) p. 6.
[2]*Employment Directions 1975* may be ordered from the National Employment Association, 2000 K Street N.W., Washington, D.C., 20006 ($3.60 Prepaid).

personnel offices, placement services, public and private employment agencies—compose only a partial outline. The list also includes many other channels to employment opportunities depending upon the type of work and the type of employment desired. For example, in some instances it might be wise to go directly to a potential employer and attempt to sell him on hiring you. In other instances, you should write directly to a firm's training division and request application forms to their training program.

If you are interested in a civil service position, for example, you will need to take a civil service test before you can be considered for jobs classified as "general service" (to level 13). For positions above a G.S. 13, you would have to write to the Civil Service regional director for the proper forms.

These examples indicate several important points. First, it is important to have a good idea of the kind of work you want to do and are capable and qualified to do. Then it is necessary to locate jobs for which you have the qualifications or can get the necessary qualifications. Then you need to discover the procedures and techniques for landing such a position. It is important to get the exact names and addresses of people who can help you to do this. Get the exact name, the spelling of that name, and the address of the person who can help you. Don't be content to speak or write to "Recruiter" or "Personnel Manager" or "President." Find out who these people are. In many cases that information is no further away than your telephone. For a more thorough discussion of these techniques, see the section in Chapter 3 on "Research: Investigating the Company."

In the following chapters we will provide you with proven and professional procedures, tips, and techniques for getting positions. No matter at what stage in your changing career (beginner or veteran) you are, you will find these ideas on writing letters of job application, application forms, and resumes important to your success. The suggestions for planning, taking part in, and evaluating employment interviews will help you (it is hoped) to the top of your first, second, only, or final professional career.

CHAPTER ONE

Preparing the Letter of Application

Preparing a letter of application is difficult and complicated. Although it is one of the most frustrating letters to write, you may, if you do your job well, find that this is the one major step that will help you to get your foot in the door. It is very common for an employer to make a decision to consider or not to consider you, based solely on the impact of your initial letter. Remember, it often precedes you; it *is* you; and you are judged by it. In preparing for this chapter the authors have drawn from twelve years' experience in helping others to prepare letters of application. Part of this experience included conducting a survey of 1,000 letters of application selected at random. This survey revealed that less than 10 percent of the letters were so well written that an employer reading them might want to interview the person on the basis of the letter alone. Approximately 25 percent were so badly written that, were it not for affirmative action policies, the employer might well have preferred to have thrown them into the nearest wastebasket. Another 25 percent were so poorly written that an employer would have considered them only if he had a serious lack of applicants. The remainder were adequately written but were unimpressive. We are confident that you selected this book because you felt you needed some kind of guidance.

In order to help you to understand what we mean when we say that over 50 percent of the letters of application are poorly written, we shall share a few selected letters with you. It is important for you to understand that each of these letters is written by someone who holds *at least* a Master's degree and in some cases a Doctor's degree. As you review these letters with us, we hope that you will see why it is that many competent persons holding degrees are among the ranks of the unemployed. It is also important for you to know that these letters are not unusual; tragically, they are all too common. These are real letters. The authors have changed the names and addresses of the applicants and other pertinent data in order to protect the identity of the writers.

EXAMPLES OF POORLY WRITTEN LETTERS [1]

See Figure 1. Yes, this letter with its multitude of mistakes is indeed a true facsimile. Is it any wonder that it might be thrown away? Should it be taken seriously? Is it worth the effort? What impression do you have of the person who wrote it? In reviewing this letter with you briefly, you will notice that it is addressed to "Chairman." For a person holding a Ph.D. in this field this is inexcusable. With a minimum of effort, this writer could have found the name of the addressee. You will also notice the typographical errors and poor examples of style. In the heading, note the utilization of the letters NY for New York. While this is correct for the U.S. ZIP code, it is not in the best style. Most certainly the omission of the periods after the N and the Y might suggest carelessness. In the heading of the letter the use of "SUNY" is incorrect. That is not the name of the institution to which this person wrote. The comma after "Dear Sir," is incorrect. Very quickly you can spot misspelled words, such as the *v* instead of the *b* in September. The authors are astonished with this letter in that the writer did attend the *four* outstanding universities listed. Certainly, if it is true that the writer has a Ph.D. and is published, one would expect a letter of much higher quality.

---

[1] All letters are true facsimiles with all names, addresses, and other data changed to protect the identities of the writers.

Received 8/15/72 MHO

August 2, 1972
New York, NY

Chairman
Speech/Theatre Dept
SUNY
Plattsburgh, NY

Dear Sir,

Will you be needing a Speech/Theatre man for this next Septemver?

I have taught at State Univ. of New York (Buffalo), Univ. of Delaware, and the City College of New York. My educational background includes Univ. of Southern Illinois, Redlands Univ., Case-Western Reserve, and New York University.

I have a PhD and am published.

Sincerely,

Martin G. Ohlson

Dr. Martin G. Ohlson

Figure 1

Letter written by Dr. Martin G. Ohlson

The letter shown in Figure 2 speaks loudly for itself. Here you see the negative results of a poorly written letter which neither identifies the position the person is seeking nor tells anything about the individual. The kindest thing that we can say about this letter is: "It would have been better had it not been written at all." Certainly, the employer does not have the time to request the vital missing data.

One of the main points that will be emphasized in this chapter is: *Your* letter reflects you. Figure 3, with its general type-written message (which in and of itself is very poor) and its large scrawling handwriting, does not make the kind of impact that you would like to make for yourself. Yes, that big circle in the middle of the page was on the letter when it arrived, as was the arrow. Perhaps you felt the same as the authors did, that this letter was written by a highly aggressive individual with a bossy nature. We may be wrong; but, since we have only the letter to do the "talking," we don't have to take the chance of finding out.

No, the publisher did not make a mistake; that's the way the letter in Figure 4 looked when we received it. It was very difficult to read: For one thing, the typewriter ribbon should have been replaced five years ago. And, yes, the keys of the type-writer did type that unevenly. Your choice of paper, your choice of typewriter, and the quality of the ribbon which you use are all important.

How much is the application shown in Figure 5 worth? Answer: Nine cents, the price of the postcard.

Notice Figure 6. The "President" is hardly the place to apply for a position. You can also see the poor impression created by combining a poorly written first sentence with a too brief *résumé*. It has been said that a picture is worth a thousand words. The authors contend that one poorly written letter, such as this, creates such a poor picture that it will receive only one word—*NO*.

We call your attention to the first sentence of the letter shown in Figure 7: "I am interested in the possibilities of a teaching position in the areas of Drama, Speech or English."

Received 11/7/73 [illegible]

Nov 1, 1973
Edina, Minn

Dear Sir,

In the event you need a teacher for spring Semester, please contact me at address below.

Yours,
Dr. Walter Wade
Box 79
Edina, Minn
16464

Figure 2
Letter written by Dr. Walter Wade

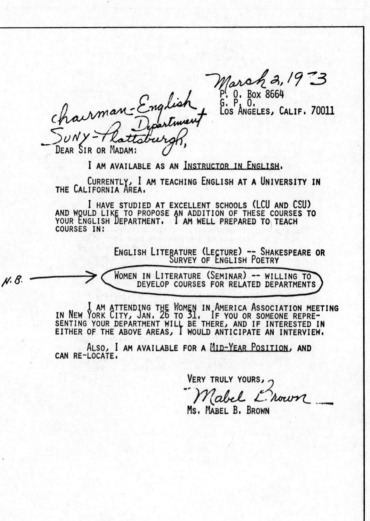

March 2, 1973
P. O. Box 8664
G. P. O.
LOS ANGELES, CALIF. 70011

chairman-English
Department
SUNY-Plattsburgh,

DEAR SIR OR MADAM:

I AM AVAILABLE AS AN <u>INSTRUCTOR IN ENGLISH</u>.

CURRENTLY, I AM TEACHING ENGLISH AT A UNIVERSITY IN THE CALIFORNIA AREA.

I HAVE STUDIED AT EXCELLENT SCHOOLS (LCU AND CSU) AND WOULD LIKE TO PROPOSE AN ADDITION OF THESE COURSES TO YOUR ENGLISH DEPARTMENT. I AM WELL PREPARED TO TEACH COURSES IN:

ENGLISH LITERATURE (LECTURE) -- SHAKESPEARE OR
SURVEY OF ENGLISH POETRY

N. B. → WOMEN IN LITERATURE (SEMINAR) -- WILLING TO
DEVELOP COURSES FOR RELATED DEPARTMENTS

I AM ATTENDING THE WOMEN IN AMERICA ASSOCIATION MEETING IN NEW YORK CITY, JAN. 26 TO 31. IF YOU OR SOMEONE REPRESENTING YOUR DEPARTMENT WILL BE THERE, AND IF INTERESTED IN EITHER OF THE ABOVE AREAS, I WOULD ANTICIPATE AN INTERVIEW.

ALSO, I AM AVAILABLE FOR A <u>MID-YEAR POSITION</u>, AND CAN RE-LOCATE.

VERY TRULY YOURS,

Mabel Brown
MS. MABEL B. BROWN

Figure 3
Letter written by Ms. Mabel B. Brown

February 11, 1971
Edwardsville, Pa.

Chairman
Speech Dept
S.U.N.Y.
Plattsburgh, N.Y.

Dear Sir,

I am presently an assoc. prof. in the
Speech Dept. at Edwardsville State College, Edwardsville,
Pa. I am desirous of spending one more year with
S.U.N.Y. (I have previously taught at Geneseo and
Stoney Brook). If you have need for a one year only
teacher in the areas of Speech/Theatre/English,
please contact me at address below.

I am usually in my office Tues-Thurs. AM,
between 10-12. Phone 664-3215, Sta. 591.

Yours truly,

Samuel M. Lowney

Dr. Samuel M. Lowney
96 David Drive
Edwardsville, Pa.

Figure 4
Letter written by Dr. Samuel M. Lowney

Chairman
Department of Speech
State University of New York
Plattsburgh, New York 12901

VACANCY INFORMATION REQUEST

Education
  BFAE   1964
  Clarkson College
  MS   1970
  Eastern Texas University

Experience
  Secondary 1964-1969
    Junior High (Texas)
    Senior High (Maryland)
  University
    Music Department (Vermont)

Proficiency
  Voice and Choral Direction
  Piano
  Music Composition

Contact: Miss Helen Wilson
          345 N. Walnut St.
          Lyndon, Vermont

Telephone: 618   653-7250

Figure 5
Vacancy Information Requested—on a Post Card

To the President:

Apt. # 35
481 E. Seventh St.
New York, N.Y. 10056
March 8th
1 9 7 2

I should like to apply for a position on your faculty.

RESUME OF TRAINING AND EXPERIENCE:

Bachelor of Arts in History, Cranford University, 1953

Master of Fine Arts in Theatre, U.C.O.C., 1961
    Thesis Subject: "Thomas Mann and the American Stage"

State of Colorado Teaching Certificate No. 21975 MWD
    with a Specialization in Community College Teaching
        Major Subject: Creative Drama
        Minor Subject: History

Special subjects: Directing, Scenic Design, Acting,
    Communication Arts, History of the
    Theatre, Modern European History,
    History of Schubert

Professional Career:

    As an Actor: on Broadway in "Streetcar Named Desire"
        1966-67 and in "Cold Steel" 1967-68

        featured in the National Company of
        "Act VVI" (starring Leslie Tucker)

        Many plays off-Broadway and in stock

        extensive television experience

    As a Director: off-Broadway, stock, and community
        theatre

        (stage name: Harry Liner)

    Member of Actors' Equity XV225, Screen Actors'
        Guild, and American Fed. of TV and Radio Artists.

Age: 40

        Telephone: 518 677-8880

            Yours very truly,

            Peter M. Cessington
            Peter M. Cessington

Figure 6
Combination Letter/Resume Addressed: "To the President"

State University at Plattsburgh
Plattsburgh
New York 12901

Dear Sirs:

      I am interested in the possibilities of a teaching position in the areas of drama, speech or English in your college for the fall of 1971. I would also be interested in a teaching appointment for a summer school session or substitute secretarial work for this summer. I have had experience in a registrar's office. Enclosed you will find a resume of my past activities and experience.

      Additional to this information. I have spent the past two years living and working in the mountains near Salt Lake City, Utah, where I co-organized a music workshop for guitar, dulcimer and autoharp. I am also presently authoring a volume of poetry.

      I would appreciate it if you would keep my resume on file or forward it to the appropriate department for consideration in case any openings should occur.

                  Sincerely yours,

                  Raymond D. Barton

                  Raymond D. Barton

enc.

Figure 7
Letter written by Raymond D. Barton

This clearly reflects an applicant who has not adequately assessed his abilities. A college graduate should know that in most universities *Drama, Speech,* and *English* represent three different major departments, or at least three distinct teaching areas. As if that isn't enough, within any one of those areas there are several different types of positions. This applicant would do well to learn the lesson of identifying *exactly* what it is for which he is qualified and for which he is applying.

Would you hire the person who wrote the letter shown in Figure 8? We wouldn't.

See the letter in Figure 9. You will be pleased to know we kept his application in the "strictest" confidence. We didn't consider it at all. There are exceptions where such a request would be taken for granted. A president of a major corporation would require complete confidentiality since any rumor of his moving could have major impact upon the companies involved, the stock market, and internal company morale.

How bad do letters get? Try the one shown in Figure 10! First, it is addressed to Potsdam but mailed to Plattsburgh; it is poorly typed on the *top* half of an old sheet of paper; the page was torn in half; and the letter itself is poor. We assume the bottom half of the page included the letter addressed to Plattsburgh but mailed to Potsdam. In addition we found one other letter with thirty-one misspelled words out of forty-two total. We have a few letters from writers who omitted postage—which then had to be paid by the employer, adding insult to injury. With the new postal policies, your application would be returned to *you*—perhaps causing you to miss the deadline.

MENTAL ATTITUDE

The major reason we included the examples which you just read was to show you what people do or fail to do which has such a devastating impact upon their chances for employment. There is no question in our minds that even if you were to stop

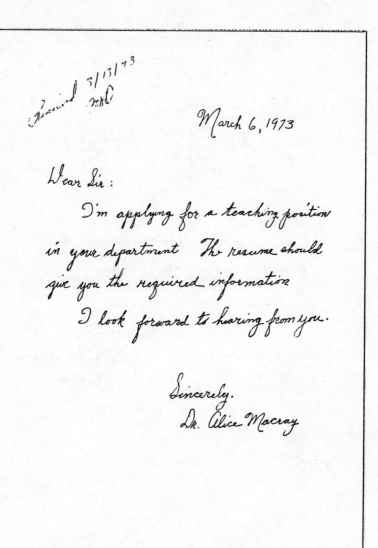

Figure 8
Letter written by Dr. Alice Macray

Box 3116
Rochester, New York 19152
11 November, 1974

My dear Sir,

    With reference to your listing I am enclosing a brief resume.

    I write in strictest confidence and I trust this will be received in that spirit. If there is any further information you wish, please let me know.

Yours truly,

John R. Colechester

John R. Colechester

CC-26
S C A

Figure 9
Letter written in "Strictest Confidence" by Colechester

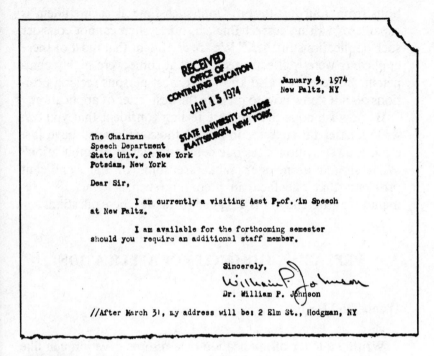

RECEIVED
OFFICE OF
CONTINUING EDUCATION
JAN 15 1974
STATE UNIVERSITY COLLEGE
PLATTSBURGH, NEW YORK

January 9, 1974
New Paltz, NY

The Chairman
Speech Department
State Univ. of New York
Potsdam, New York

Dear Sir,

   I am currently a visiting Asst Prof. in Speech at New Paltz.

   I am available for the forthcoming semester should you require an additional staff member.

        Sincerely,

        Dr. William P. Johnson

//After March 31, my address will be: 2 Elm St., Hodgman, NY

Figure 10
Letter written by Dr. William P. Johnson on a torn half sheet of paper

reading this book right now, you would not make the kinds of mistakes that you just witnessed. Your awareness is "up"; your attention has been called to the importance of care in better writing. Having used these examples in numerous public presentations, we know that your attitude is one of astonishment and disbelief—astonishment and disbelief that *anyone* could write letters such as these. The authors make no pretense that they know all of the writers of these letters; however, we do know that the writers were highly educated persons. We also assure you that employers concur with our findings that numerous applicants cannot (do not) prepare an adequate letter of application. One superintendent of a northern New York school system returned over fifty letters to a major university with the following note: "Enclosed are the current job applications from your institution. Until such time as each student is capable of writing correct English, our system cannot consider such applications further." We are confident that most of these applicants were well educated and that some were highly competent; however, we also know that most persons seeking positions do not know how to prepare the best letter of application.

By now we hope that you are feeling confident that you *can* write a letter far superior to any of those which you have just read. However, how does one compose a letter of application? What should it include? What are some of the significant problems that one faces in preparing such a letter? The remainder of this chapter is designed to answer these questions.

PREPARING THE LETTER OF APPLICATION

Where Do I Begin?

Writing a letter of application or a résumé is very much like writing a major report or a difficult paper. Very few people are such accomplished writers and so well organized that they can begin composing before doing some research, gathering various materials and ideas, and carefully organizing their thoughts. It is also important to know that the letter(s) you are writing must provide attractive, sufficient information which will win you the opportunity for obtaining a personal interview. It should not be too long nor should it attempt to be an autobiography. Let's consider the letter of application in two stages: first, an appropriate format reflecting how your final product might look; and secondly, the specifics of the content itself.

Make a Good Beginning Impression

The ancient Greeks had a term called *ethos*. This term means the manner in which the person reading your letter (or speaking with you) is impressed by *you*. In your case, your *ethos* is affected by the quality of the paper you choose, by the quality of your typewriter, and by the quality of the ribbon with which you type, as well as by the total impact that the final letter makes upon the reader. Of course, what you say and how you say it is the essence. A letter of application represents you as if you were a soldier standing at attention ready for inspection. If you are to "pass," each detail must be its best. What are the essential ingredients of a well-written letter of application? At the very beginning we recommend that you go to your nearest book or stationery store and purchase as many sheets as you feel necessary of a good quality bond paper. This paper should be twenty pound weight and at least a twenty-five percent rag content. The manager of the store will be able to tell you what we mean by a quality rag bond paper if you do not know. He will also have a variety which will provide you with a choice. This kind of paper has a beautiful hard finish which takes ink well. It looks very white and is as impressive as a fine piece of stationery. Next, we recommend that you arrange to have your letter and *résumé* typed on an electric typewriter with a modern type face. Do avoid *script* or *italic* type faces. Select a typewriter which uses a carbon ribbon (sometimes known as a "once-through" ribbon). This type of ribbon makes a sharp, glossy, *printed* look; and when typed on the paper we recommended, the result is quite impressive. Finally, we recommend that you follow an excellent format, that is, how your letter is set upon the page. The examples which we will review with you in the next few pages are all written in acceptable formats. We do caution you, though, that there is no one correct format and no one correct way. You, the reader, should select the format that best serves your needs for the particular position for which you are applying.

Organization and Details Are Important

The time you spend now, in attending to details, will be returned to you many times over in the time and frustration you save in seeking *that* position. This section explains significant details regarding: 1) the heading, 2) the inside address, 3) the greeting or salutation, 4) the body, 5) the closing, and 6) the signature.

THE HEADING

The first consideration of the letter of application is the heading, which is composed of the return address and the date. Most of us are quite familiar with the heading which is typed about five to fifteen spaces from the top of the page in the top right hand corner of the page. The heading you see in the letter addressed to Mr. Carl C. Jones (in Figure 11) provides a good example. The return address, 27 McDonough Street, Plattsburgh, New York 12901; and the date, May 3, 1973, are spaced correctly. If you so choose, it would be equally correct to type the return address and the date immediately above "Mr. Carl C. Jones" and flush with the left-hand margin. There should be five spaces between the heading and the inside address. It is important that you include your return address if you expect a reply. Nearly all words in a letter of application are spelled out and you should avoid abbreviations. The letter of application is a formal letter and it is imperative that you attempt to be complete and thorough. This includes correctly spelled words, well-written sentences, and a demonstration that you have an adequate command of English.

INSIDE ADDRESS

Returning to the letter in Figure 11, the second major part of that letter is the *inside address,* "Mr. Carl C. Jones, Director of Personnel, National Casualty, Inc., 410 South Illinois Avenue, Chicago, Illinois, 60606." This is a well-written inside address in that it includes the name of the person to whom you are writing, his title, the correct name of the company, and the correct address of the company, as well as the city, state, and the correct ZIP code. The "Inc." is correct since *Incorporated* is a long word which would look awkward if extended into the middle of the letter. You may be wondering where to find specific information such as the name of the Director of

27 MacDonough Street
Plattsburgh, New York 12901
May 3, 1973

Mr. Carl C. Jones
Director of Personnel
National Casualty, Inc.
410 South Illinois Avenue
Chicago, Illinois   60606

Dear Mr. Jones:

The reputation and growth of National Casualty, Incorporated
has led me to inquire whether new positions may be developing
in your claims department. I am interested in the possibility
of an accounting position beginning in June, 1974.

In May, 1974, I will be completing four years service in the
United States Air Force as a legal services specialist. My
field of specialization during this time has been in claims.

The past two years have provided me experience in the investigation and adjudication of claims. My initial duties as a
claims examiner in 1971 were enhanced the following year when I
became the non-commissioned officer in charge of claims at the
Plattsburgh Air Force Base. During this time academic endeavors
in accounting complimented this experience. A second Bachelor
of Science degree in accounting will be received in May, 1974.
I received my first degree in mathematics in 1970.

Enclosed is a copy of my resume. I would be happy to provide
you with my complete dosier from the Marion State College Placement Service along with any material or information you might
request. I can be available for an interview at our mutual
convenience.

Thank you for your consideration.

Sincerely,

Charles L. Evans

enc.

Figure 11
Letter to Mr. Carl C. Jones

Personnel. The *Introduction* discusses where to seek employment opportunities and how to find this type of information.

Salutation or Greeting

The salutation, "Dear Mr. Jones:" is correct. Of course, if you did not know his name it would be correct to begin, "Dear Sir:". However, knowing the name makes a much greater impression. Both "Dear Mr. Jones" and "Dear Sir" are followed by a colon(:). This is the *only* punctuation mark following the salutation which is correct in a formal letter of application. The comma, which is incorrect in this case, is only used when you know the person to whom you are writing in a personal letter.

The Body

The body of the letter may take several forms, depending upon your level of experience, the type of position you are seeking, and many other questions which we will cover in this text. Essentially, there are two major ways of organizing the letter of application. The methods represented in Figures 11 and 12 show the most useful models for the majority of applicants. Remember, the end product is your letter, your image; and the final format, of necessity, must be your decision.

Paragraph 1. The first paragraph of the letter of application is without a doubt the most difficult for most applicants to compose; and yet it is the most important paragraph to write and one which should follow proper guidelines. Specifically, there are at least three requirements which could be included in the first paragraph:

1. What motivated me to write the letter to this specific source?
2. Exactly what is it for which I am applying?
3. Is it clear what I have to offer or can do for *each* company?

Some employers want applicants to begin immediately with what the applicant has to offer to or can do for the company.

Star Route Box 70
Peru, New York

January 22, 1975

Mr. David L. James
Inter American World Airways, Inc.
1325 North Pacific Avenue
Palm Beach, Florida

Dear Mr. James:

I have received information that the International Services Division of Inter American World Airways, Incorporated is bidding on logistics support at Kwajalein, Marshall Islands. Since my interests and skills are in management and aviation related positions, I would appreciate your consideration for the position of Pilot and supervisory or management responsibilities.

Effective June 30, 1975, I shall complete twenty-one years service in the United States Air Force. Relocation and job commencement would be possible the following month. I hold the military ratings of Command Pilot and Navigator. My Federal Aviation Administration Commercial Pilot Certificate, Number 0035059 includes the ratings of: airplane single and multi-engine land, rotorcraft-helicopter, and instrument, including helicopter.

During the past nineteen years, I have accumulated over five thousand hours of flying time. Included in this time are seven hundred fifty hours of helicopter pilot time and three hundred hours of performing duties as a navigator. I have seventy-six trans-oceanic flights as an Aircraft Commander. Since 1967, I have performed instructor pilot duties in B-58, HH-53 and FB-111 military aircraft. Positions which I have held include Director of Training, Chief Standardization Division, and Chief Training Devices Branch. My special interests are in the field of flight simulation and flight instruction. As Chief Training Devices Branch, I supervised seventy simulator technicians and managed thirty-five million dollars of flight simulator equipment.

Attached is a resume for your convenience. Military records and credentials may be obtained by contacting the Director of Personnel, 380 Combat Support Group, Plattsburgh Air Force Base, New York 12903. I am willing to provide any additional information you may need and I am available for an interview at your convenience.

Thank you for your consideration.

Sincerely yours,

Jonathan Bellaire

Jonathan Bellaire

Figure 12
Letter to Mr. David L. James

25

The authors believe that this is an effective opening for experienced, confident applicants. We do caution that you do not appear overly aggressive or overbearing. An opening such as "My analytical skills and research abilities in the areas of computer programming may be of significant interest to you" is an effective beginning which presents a confident applicant directly to the employer. Equally as effective would be an opening which begins: "The enclosed résumé highlights my experience as a successful, innovative analyst and researcher in computer programming." There are other effective means for beginning which must be evaluated carefully.

Interspersed are three sample letters. Turning to the letter addressed to Mr. Carl C. Jones (Figure 11), the opening paragraph begins, "The reputation and growth of National Casualty, Incorporated has led me to inquire whether new positions may be developing in your claims department." The impetus or the motivation for writing this sentence becomes quite clear. This minimally experienced young man is not certain whether or not this large corporation has a position or not. This type of opening is called a *blind lead*. It is an acceptable opening when writing to a company with potential openings at any time. One can thus anticipate that within a given year such an opening might well occur. You must exercise caution not to send letters in a "shot gun" manner to large numbers of companies. Be selective. In Figure 12, written by an experienced manager, we have what is called a "known lead," where the letter states, "I have received information. . . ." This letter could be improved in view of today's requirements of Affirmative Action had the writer stated the source of his information. For example, "The January 22, 1976 issue of the *New York Times* lists . . . ." Today, many corporations that advertise do want to know how effective their advertisements are, and they are expected to keep records stating where prospective employees gained the information. If you learned of the position from an employee of the company, we do not recommend that you use that employee's name unless he has specifically given you permission to do so. After all, he is an employee of the company, not the director of placement; and you may cause him significant embarrassment.

This situation is probably best handled by using a blind lead such as: "It has been brought to my attention that a possible opening for . . . ."

Figure 13, written by an experienced educator, sets an excellent tone for the letter and clearly delineates the motivation for writing. It also provides the source and specifically identifies the position for which the person is applying when it states, "I would appreciate your consideration as a candidate for the position of Dean, College of Humanities, Arts and Social Sciences as delineated in *The Chronicle*." Each of these three openings illustrates the need to state what has motivated the applicant to write. But more importantly for you, the applicant, this is a logical, simple way for you to begin the letter. There are many other ways for you to begin. For example, if you were interested in a particular area of the country you might begin, "In as much as I am interested in obtaining a position in the Roanoke, Virginia area . . . ." Another example with which one might begin is: "Effective February 1, 1976, I shall be completing my career commitment with the United States Army and am interested in . . . ." A potential high school or college graduate might adapt a similar opening to read: "Effective June 1, 1976, I anticipate completing all requirements for graduation with a Regents' Diploma from Lincoln-Way High School in Dexter, New York. I am interested in . . . ." The key to remember in selecting your first sentence is to be sincere and honest.

The second major point which should go into the opening paragraph is to state what it is for which you are applying. Figure 11 states, "I am interested in the possibility of an accounting position . . . ." This concise statement clearly states exactly what this applicant is applying for. It leaves little question or doubt. Just prior to this statement, the applicant defined it more concisely when he wrote, " . . . led me to inquire whether new positions may be developing in your claims department." This is a good illustration of how a relatively inexperienced applicant might state succinctly what it is for which he is applying. Take caution to be clear about the position in which you are interested; however, you must be careful not to be so general that the employer has little knowledge of what you seek. Being

2 James Place South
Plattsburgh, New York 12901

October 3, 1975

Dean Norman A. Smith
Chairman, Search Committee
School of Graduate Studies
State University of America
Logan, Utah 84322

Dear Dean Smith:

I would appreciate your consideration as a candidate for the position of Dean, College of Humanities, Arts and Social Sciences as delineated in The Chronicle.

Presently, I am beginning my seventh year with the State University of New York College of Arts and Science at Plattsburgh. During this period I have served as a tenured professor of communications, departmental chairman, chairman of the Faculty Senate, President of the A.A.U.P., and, at the request of the President, Coordinator of General Studies which includes both the B.A. and the M.A. interdisciplinary degrees.

I am most interested in the position of Dean at State University of America because it does offer an opportunity for a new administrative challenge and personal growth in a community similar to Plattsburgh -- both are centers of major winter recreational areas with the types of family activities we enjoy. I am confident that your committee will find me to be a dedicated teacher-administrator who offers the following characteristics and abilities:

1. A strong, proven motivation to excel consistently as a teacher and as an administrator. During the past ten years I have received recognition as an outstanding teacher by graduate and undergraduate students as well as a special commendation for outstanding service to the Faculty from the Faculty Senate last year.

2. A desire to strengthen existing programs and to develop new concepts. Currently, I have had the pleasure to contribute to the implementation of numerous programs and concepts which have had major impact on our university -- concepts and programs such as both undergraduate and graduate degrees in Speech Pathology/Audiology, three separate $100,000 contracts in Leadership and Communication with the Air Force, an extensive B.A. as well as an M.A. degree program of an interdisciplinary nature, and a revision of the Faculty Bylaws.

3. An effective communicator -- most capable of communicating with the student body, the faculty, the administration, and with the broad public a university serves.

Figure 13
Letter to Dean Smith

4. The ability to set both short and long-ranged goals for both myself and for the duties expected of me. In this sense, I consider my ability to motivate others and to instill a strong sense of responsibility and rapport most significant.

5. The ability to think a problem through which includes a desire to establish priorities, to do the necessary "homework", and to consult all parties with a significant interest in the problem.

6. A broad scope of interests and abilities which, I believe, provide an adequate basis for a genuine and lasting interest in the position of Dean -- You will find me ready to serve and to support as needed.

Having just served on the Search Committees for both a new President and for a Vice President of Academic Affairs, I know the extensive work your committee faces. If the above philosophy and the attached credentials are not descriptive of the person you seek, just say so; and, you may be certain that my attitude would be to wish the successful candidate God speed.

Attached are the names of references and a rather comprehensive <u>Vitae</u>. You may contact anyone at my present college. If there is any other information which you might desire, I am willing to provide it.

Thank you for your consideration.

Sincerely,

DR. WILLIAM M. CLARK

Figure 13
(continued)

29

too concise may also be detrimental. The applicant in Figure 11 may be narrowing himself too far by specifying the "claims department." It is quite possible that the company might have an accounting position open in a variety of departments such as auditing or payroll.

In the letter addressed to Mr. James (Figure 12), you see a person with extensive experience applying for an advanced position. The last sentence in his opening paragraph states, "Since my interests and skills are in management and aviation related positions, I would appreciate your consideration for the position of Pilot with supervisory or management responsibilities." As in Figure 11, this is a concise statement of what it is that this applicant wants to do. It leaves no doubt in the mind of the reader. When the specific position is provided in a job description or advertisement, do use that description in your letter. Such a statement should not exceed one sentence.

In reviewing the opening paragraph, it is important once again to stress that the easiest way for you to begin is to begin with that which motivated you to write the letter in the first place. You have these examples to follow; however, remember our words of caution: Use them as examples only. An opening which introduces you and your purpose well is of special value to the employer in that he or she can read it quickly and determine immediately whether or not there is a position for which you might be qualified. It saves the employer valuable time in trying to read through a less well written letter. Our goal is to help you to write a letter in such a way that anyone reading it will want to read each succeeding paragraph, and, ultimately, to meet you in an interview.

Paragraph 2. Paragraph two and paragraph three can represent a one-two punch within your letter. Paragraph two should serve as a general summary of your education, experience, or other general areas of significance which should be shared with the prospective employer. Reviewing Figure 11, we read, "In May, 1974, I will be completing four years service in the United States Air Force as a legal services specialist. My field of specialization during this time has been in claims." This second paragraph is excellent for a young man with relatively limited experience. It is also the type of paragraph which a graduating high school senior or a student about to complete his college education might write. In Figure 12 we read, "I hold the military ratings of Command Pilot and Navigator, my Federal Aviation Administration Commercial Pilot Certificate, Number 0035059 includes the ratings of: airplane single and multi-engine land, rotorcraft-helicopter, and instrument, including helicopter." This provides the busy executive who is probably reading this letter with most adequate information to aid in determining the general qualifications of this experienced applicant.

In Figure 13, the reader will find a different approach. Thus, let's hold it in abeyance until we complete our discussion of the total letter of application.

Paragraph 3. Paragraph three is an amplification of paragraph two in that it provides more detailed illustration of the applicant's background and experience. For an experienced person, there are three points which this paragraph should definitely stress. First, if you are an experienced applicant, you should state any experience that you have had in working with human resources (either supervising people or working with others as an organizational leader). Secondly, you should state any experience which you have had in working with material resources (budgeting, financial management). Finally, you should include a sufficiently detailed description of your responsibilities or duties. For the less experienced applicant, you may use these same points but draw upon your experiences with student groups, athletics, community activities, offices you might have held, scholastic record (illustrates how well you carried out your "duties" as a student), or with work. No work experience is insignificant; so do not hold yourself in low esteem.

In Figure 11 we read:

The past two years have provided me experience in the investigation and adjudication of claims. My initial duties as a claims examiner in 1971 were enhanced the following year when I became the non-commissioned officer in charge of claims at the Plattsburgh Air Force Base. During this time academic endeavors in accounting complemented this experience. A second Bachelor of Science degree in accounting will be received in May, 1974.

This is a young man with two years experience which he describes simply and concisely. He makes no claims that he is a highly experienced manager; he merely states that he was the non-commissioned officer in charge of claims. In this position he might perhaps have had two or three younger persons working with him. Most significant is the fact that here is a "go-getter"; he is not content just to do his job but wants to improve himself. We see this revealed in the fact that he is working on an additional college degree. For the reader who is a high school student or a college student, it could be wise to include some type of statement within your letter that indicates a willingness to continue your education or a willingness to enter training or apprentice programs.

In the more advanced letter, illustrated in Figure 12, the reader sees that the applicant delineates his 5,000 hours of flying time and then the specifics of that flying time. The facts are impressive: 750 hours in helicopters and 300 hours in performing the duties of the navigator, in addition to other extensive experiences, such as his 76 trans-oceanic flights as a commander. Finally, his last sentence illustrates the two points which we suggest the experienced person stress, "As Chief, Training Devices Branch, I supervised seventy simulator technicians and managed thirty-five million dollars of flight simulator equipment." This statement clearly says that the writer has had experience in supervising human resources as well as experience in the supervision of material resources. The remainder of that paragraph amplifies these two criteria by spelling out what his specific duties and responsibilities were. Thus, paragraph two and three serve as that one-two punch. Paragraph two, a concise general overview of your background, experiences, and education; paragraph three, more specifically, an amplification of your background and experience.

Paragraph 4. Paragraph four serves as a summary statement to your letter of application. It contains that type of essential information which an employer will want to know for an oral interview or prior to employing you. The types of information which this paragraph might include are: a résumé; a list of your references; a sentence stating that you are willing to provide the employer with any other materials which he might need; and a statement that you are available for an interview. If you are already employed, such as in the Military, you should state that you are available for an interview "at our mutual convenience," which tells the employer that you may have to make arrangements in order to come.

There are a select few people such as writers, artists, or musicians who would want to state that they also have a portfolio available or that they are willing to come for an audition. A portfolio is a valuable document and would include examples or photographs of a person's work. For example, a newspaper reporter might have a portfolio of the different types of stories he has written. This might even be true for a high school or college student who has done significant writing; or, for the artist, a portfolio would be a photograph collection or a few representative examples of that artist's work carefully presented in a portfolio collection. The applicant should never send the portfolio unless it is specifically requested; and, even then, there are serious precautions necessary, such as using registered mail and providing sufficient return postage. The portfolio will be discussed more fully in the chapter on special problems.

Following the fourth paragraph is a most important statement which so many writers omit. Nothing flowery but short, concise and to the point should be a simple "thank you," or "thank you for your consideration." The applicant is cautioned to avoid any type of statement that might alienate the person reading his letter—such as "I hope to hear from you soon," "I hope to hear from you at your very earliest convenience," or "I trust that you will keep this in the very strictest of confidence." Even though you may not intend to be hostile, such statements are often perceived in that way. Proofread your completed letter carefully (we urge you to do so aloud); and be certain that you have not included anything which would be better omitted or which is in error.

One question that many applicants ask us is, "What should I do about salary?" Unless you have been asked to respond definitely to this question or unless there is some aspect which is an absolute requisite to you, it is our recommendation that you reserve any discussion of salary until the employer asks you such a specific question, either in an application form or in the oral interview. Again, questions of salary will be discussed in a later chapter.

THE SIGNATURE

Every typed letter of application should provide ample space for both a typed and signed signature. Although you may pride yourself on your excellent handwriting, you may learn that others cannot read it as well.

An Alternative Approach

Figure 13 represents an alternative approach for the experienced applicant. Paragraphs one and two are essentially the same as those in Figures 11 and 12. The major difference is in the delineation of experience and what this person feels he can do. Paragraph three states, "I am most interested in the position of Dean at State University of America because it does offer an opportunity for a new administrative challenge and personal growth in a community similar to Plattsburgh—both are centers of major winter recreational areas with the types of family activities we enjoy." This goes beyond being a statement of motivation. It specifically tells the reader that this applicant is looking for a new administrative challenge, and that he is seeking a position in a community quite similar to the one in which he currently lives. The last sentence in that paragraph, "I am confident that your committee will find me to be a dedicated teacher-administrator who offers the following characteristics and abilities:" represents an attitude which is positive; that is, here is a person who believes in his abilities and who has a confident attitude. It also points out that he has two major attributes: He is a teacher and he is an administrator. What kind of teacher and administrator is he? The remainder of the letter illustrates a significant departure from that in Figures 11 and 12. The reader will note that there are six numbered criteria. Each of these criteria is a performance objective by which an employer may evaluate an employee or an applicant. This writer has reversed the role and has applied the criteria to himself. Of course, he is confident that his references will support his own evaluation. Point one in his letter states, "A strong proven motivation to excel consistently as a teacher and as an administrator." This statement represents a *criterion*. The applicant is saying that if you are seeking a person who has the ability to motivate and to excel consistently as a teacher and as an administrator, then I am that type of person. The remainder of that part illustrates that the applicant is not content to imply that he can do this but that he offers evidence to support it. Notice this sentence: "During the past ten years I have received recognition as an outstanding teacher by graduate and undergraduate students as well as a special commendation for outstanding service to the faculty from the Faculty Senate last year." Obviously, such documentation clearly establishes that we have a person with significant administrative and teaching background. The remainder of the points follow a similar pattern.

The experienced applicant in any field is encouraged to examine the six criteria: a strong, proven motivation to excel consistently; a desire to strengthen existing programs and to develop new concepts; proven ability as an effective communicator; the ability to set both short and long-ranged goals; the ability to think a problem through, which includes a desire to establish priorities, to do the necessary homework, and to consult all parties with significant interest in the problem; and a broad scope of interests and abilities.

These six aspects or performance objectives help provide an employer with a method by which he can assess the needs of the position which he might have open, and a method by which he can evaluate the effectiveness of an employee once he hires him. The applicant who wrote the letter in Figure 13 indicates that he is an experienced administrator and can meet such performance objectives. There are many other variations which an applicant can follow. The three letters which have been presented here are not intended to be used as specific models; they are intended to provide you with insights into what others have done. In your case we urge you to re-read these letters, to re-read the criteria for the various paragraphs, and to compose your own letter carefully and with as much skill as you can. If you do this, we are confident that the final letter of application will reflect your strength as an applicant.

The Most Important Letter of All?

After you have written your letter of application, mailed it, and anxiously awaited responses from the various employers to whom you may have sent it, it is time to contemplate your next step. It is our recommendation that, if you receive a response that says, "Sorry," you respond with a brief letter of thank you expressing your appreciation for the prompt response and for considering your application. Obviously, if the response says, "Yes, we are interested in you, would like to arrange for an interview, and would like you to provide additional data," then we recommend that you sit down immediately and send a letter saying thank you for your prompt response and informing the prospective employer that you are completing the forms and will return them at your earliest convenience.

Figure 14 is the only letter of thank you which the authors found in their survey of 1,000 letters. You, the reader, can see the impression that it makes. Yes, we would want to hire this type of person. Again, we caution you: You must be sincere, and you must be concise.

```
                              1428 Miller Road
                              Athens, Georgia
                                 30601


        January 6, 1972


        Dr. Charles D. White
        Department of Art
        State University College
           at Plattsburgh
        Plattsburgh, New York

        Dear Dr. White:

        Thank you very much for your letter of January fourth.

        I appreciate your consideration, and am pleased that
        you have forwarded my letter and curriculum vitae to
        your newly elected chairman, Dr. Swinyer.

        Again, thank you for your concern.

        Sincerely,


        Keith C. Hanson
```

Figure 14
Thank you letter to Dr. Charles D. White

Some Guidelines

In concluding this chapter, we have prepared a checklist of
dos and don'ts. We urge you to use it as an overview of what
we consider the important points in this chapter, as well as a

checklist in evaluating your letter of application. You will also find three additional letters that represent variations in style from that already discussed.

Figure 15 represents a highly experienced, confident programmer using a blind approach forcefully but positively. This successful letter meets the criteria discussed earlier but provides the reader with a different perspective to gain an employer's attention. Be positive but be careful not to appear too aggressive.

Figure 16 represents an inexperienced younger person applying for a traineeship using a strong, positive approach. The confidence demonstrated is unusual for such an applicant and should create a favorable image. With modification this style could serve an experienced person's purpose.

Figure 17 represents an experienced person desiring a different position due to internal reorganization. This style can be modified by an applicant who may have been retrenched or "riffed." The organizational pattern introduces the applicant and describes his current status and motivation.

In reviewing this chapter, we hope that you have acquired insights into how to prepare your own successful letter.

CHECK LIST OF POTENTIAL DOS AND DON'TS
FOR LETTER OF APPLICATION

This check list can be helpful as you begin to write your letter of application and as a review after you have completed it. Not all the items are necessarily applicable to your letter.

Materials   Select quality paper and a good typewriter with a quality ribbon. If possible, use same type paper for letter as for résumé.

```
                                2031 East Arnold
                                Norfolk, Virginia 02330
                                February 6, 1976


    Mr. Townsend L. Manning
    General Manager
    National Rubber, Inc.
    Mobile, Alabama 23312

    Dear Mr. Manning:

    My analytical abilities in the areas of electronic data
    processing and computer programming could be of significant
    interest to you.

    Much of my current success can be attributed to my capabil-
    ity to seek out a problem, arrive at a solution, and apply
    the results for efficient and profitable management use.

    Supported with a B.S. degree in Computer Technology and a
    M.S. degree in Computer Science and Statistics, my records
    establish that I have the initiative, temperament, creativ-
    ity, and drive necessary to become a meaningful, contributing
    member of your staff.

    My resume is enclosed for your reference.  I would appreciate
    the opportunity to meet with you and to explore our mutual
    interests.  Also, I am willing to provide you any other
    information you may need as well as highest personal references.

    Thank you.


                        Very truly yours,


                        Charles J. Fox


    CJF/bg
```

Figure 15
Letter by Charles J. Fox

```
                                        641 South Maple
                                        Toronto
                                        Province of Ontario
                                        March 12, 1976




Mrs. Grace B. Connors
Director of Personnel
Millbrook Department Stores, Inc.
2000 Outer Drive
Toronto, Ontario

Dear Mrs. Connors:

     In the advent that Millbrook Department Stores need a
management trainee with proven potential, I would appreciate
consideration for such an opportunity.

     Effective June 1, 1976, I shall complete my A.S. degree
with u major in management.  During my academic career I
have maintained a high "B" average and have established my
potential for responsibility by serving as a part-time
administrative assistant to the Executive Vice President of
Bradford Business School.  This experience is supplemented
by four summers' employment as a cashier and hostess with
Vacation Inn.  My ability to work well with people and my
personal desire to excel coupled with my education and
experience should support my potential for a management
trainee position.

     I am willing to meet with you at your convenience and
to provide you with any information you may require.
References will be supplied upon request.

     Thank you for your consideration.


                              Sincerely,



                              Miss Mary J. Niles


encs.
```

Figure 16
Letter by Miss Mary J. Niles

```
                                        9 Lakeshore Drive
                                        Lakeview, New York 10861
                                        November 12, 1975


        Dr. Roger B. Culverson, President-
        Washington University
        4000 Alaska Boulevard
        Washington, District of Columbia 00011

        Dear Dr. Culverson:

        Presently, I am Dean of the Division of Fine Arts and Humanities
        at State University College of Arts and Sciences at Lakeview.
        In this position I am responsible for one hundred twenty
        faculty in eighteen departments with over 1,500 student majors.

        Due to major reorganization and consolidation, my division and
        four others will be regrouped and reassigned under the direction
        of three administrators.  As the youngest of these administrators,
        I am to be reassigned as Assistant to the President and Professor
        of Mathematics.  I prefer to remain in full-time administration
        and to function working with the challenges provided by direct
        policy involvement with faculty and students.  I desire to be
        considered as a candidate for the position of Dean of Arts and
        Sciences at Washington University.

        Attached is a copy of my Curriculum Vitae for your consideration.
        I am willing to supply you with any other information you may
        request as well as excellent references.  I can be contacted at
        my office phone (518-996-2098) or at my home phone (518-995-3034).

        Thank you.


                                Very truly yours,



                                Dr. Adam S. Webster


        encs.
```

Figure 17

Letter by Dr. Adam S. Webster

Return Address Include at least street, city, state and ZIP code. Avoid abbreviations. Avoid an address with just a Box number.

Date Do include.

Inside Address Be complete. Make effort to include addressee's name and title. Also include name of company, street, city, state, and ZIP code.

Salutation Make every effort to begin with addressee's name. If unavailable, use "Dear Sir:" Use only the colon (:) after salutation.

Content of Body Consider the following:
—Motivation for writing
—Statement of specific position for which you are applying
—Provide insights into experience and qualifications; perhaps, focus on current position and strengths
—Establish your proven potential
—Include education as a positive supplement to experience
—Meet specific criteria listed in the job advertisement
—Reflect your ability to work with human resources, financial and material resources
—State availability to come for an interview
—Avoid salary issue unless requested
—State date of availability (or omit)
—Mention any enclosures such as résumé

Additional Considerations

Do	Do Not
Be positive and reflect your your personality.	Be aggressive or over-bearing.
Type unless requested to write.	Include the name of anyone recommending you unless given permission.
Include a typed signature and sign your name.	Rely on others to mail your letter, transcripts, or application form.
Consider affirmative action requirements.	Include picture unless a definite requirement of position.
Address envelope the same as the inside address.	Use your company's stationery to apply elsewhere.
Remember to include correct postage.	Use novel approaches.
Review for correct spelling, typographical errors, and and correct English.	Use colored paper or ribbons.
Proofread aloud.	Mention personal problems unless they impede working ability.
	Tell why you are leaving a position.
	Make any negative comments regarding previous employer.

CHAPTER TWO

Preparing the Résumé

Who are you?

What are your assets?

What have you done?

What type of position do you desire?

What do you know?

Based on your résumé, would you employ yourself if you were the employer?

In Chapter One, "Preparing the Letter of Application," we pointed out that this was your opportunity to get your "foot in the door." Your résumé goes hand in glove with your letter of application. A résumé is a vehicle providing a prospective employer with many types of information about you. Résumés help to sell the most important product you have—yourself. Some authors state that not everyone needs a résumé; however, we believe that a résumé can be a very valuable asset for any serious job applicant. Whether you are a high school graduate or a highly seasoned manager, a résumé can be most valuable in providing a prospective employer with a concise outline of your attributes.

For the professional and managerial applicant, considerable attention must be given to the résumé as an important tool in seeking that high level position which will offer the opportunity for self-actualization and years of rewarding employment. For readers such as those completing a career in the military or civil service and contemplating a second career, a résumé is absolutely essential. Résumés depict attributes and assets. The résumé is often the deciding factor in determining whether or not the job seeker gets the interview with the employer. Place yourself in the role of the interviewer. An employer advertising in the *Wall Street Journal* can anticipate over 600 responses for any significant position. Confronted with the possibility of even 100 or 200 applications, we are confident that you, too, would select to interview those five or ten who have made the best impression in writing. The purpose of this chapter is to provide you with a guide to help you evaluate your "selling points" and to present them in such a manner that the impression you make on a prospective employer results in your selection for the final interview. Realistically, all you can anticipate from a letter of application and résumé is that opportunity for a face-to-face interview.

WHAT IS A RÉSUMÉ?

Whether you are seeking your first position or have a long distinguished career, the function of a résumé is to provide a particular employer with a concise summary of your personal attributes, your education, and your qualifications for a particular position. Briefly defined, résumé means summary of your life. For people within the field of education, a résumé is also referred to as a curriculum vita—a summary of your teaching (life) career.

WHY A RÉSUMÉ?

The purpose of a résumé is to provide you with an opportunity to organize the relevant facts about yourself in a concise written presentation. In this respect it must contain brief but sufficient information which will help a prospective employer to know:

Who are you?

What can you do?

What have you done?

What is your present status?

What kind of a job would you like?

What are your goals and objectives?

What are your special assets or attributes?

In presenting such an outline of your background, you will accomplish several objectives:

1. Most of us who have been employed for several years have not taken the time to evaluate our assets. Although résumé writing may be a tedious, time-consuming process, you will find it to your advantage to take this opportunity to evaluate yourself. This will help you to identify your strengths and hidden assets as well as some areas which need improvement. Thus, the self-evaluation aspect of preparing a résumé makes the effort worthwhile even though you may not use the résumé in the actual employment process. The authors believe that any person should sit down at least every two to five years and evaluate himself. Keep such evaluations current. We even recommend careful long-range planning. Where do you want to be in your career in five years? Ten? Do you need additional education or training to achieve that goal? If so, are you "programming" it into your schedule? Are you taking advantage of training programs or seminars, conferences, organizations, national meetings? Are you gaining the "right" kinds of experience and visibility?

2. A well prepared résumé will save you time by eliminating purposeless interviews.

3. A well prepared résumé will provide an employer with a focus to help him to prepare for the personal interview. Your résumé will provide him with insights that will help him phrase questions determining whether or not you are the best qualified person for the position which is available. It also helps him to help you. Quite frankly, when you have taken the time required

to organize your attributes and assets on paper you will find it much easier to discuss them with an interviewer. You will find that you have already considered, in preparing your résumé, many of the questions which he will ask. Such ready, well-organized answers will help you to have confidence and to reflect poise and maturity.

4. A major attribute of preparing a résumé is to help you to have a realistic evaluation of yourself. Such an evaluation will help you to be confident that you are neither underselling nor overselling yourself.

5. An impressive, well-written résumé serves several functions: It helps you to formulate your job objectives; it helps you to summarize your experiences and talents which may have been forgotten or minimized; it provides you with the opportunity to document/support your ability to meet your goals; it provides an initial impression to an employer which helps him to determine whether he even wants to interview you; it provides him with a visual reminder of how you "think" and with a sample of the type of work that he can anticipate from you; and it provides him with an image of you to which he can refer after the interview is completed. That could be the critical time when he makes the decision as to which of the final applicants to employ.

HOW DOES ONE PREPARE A RÉSUMÉ?

In helping you to prepare a résumé, this section will use three résumés as examples.[1] By reviewing each of these, we will provide you with insights into evaluating yourself and into what types of information you may want to include. In addition, several sample résumés are included in Appendix A with comments for your reference.

[1] All résumés are facsimiles with all names, addresses, and other data changed to protect the identities of the writers.

It is quite important to state again that, like your letter of application, your résumé must reflect you! We strongly urge you *not* to select one of the résumés presented in this book and make *you* fit *it*. Each of the résumés used as illustrations in this book is strictly for your reference, to give you ideas. Although each of the included résumés may have been satisfactory for the person for whom it was written, it is not necessarily satisfactory for you.

During our several years in helping people to prepare résumés, we have taken great pains to insure that the final product represented the person we helped and was not one prepared by us. We have confined our roles to giving advice, to helping to "pull" the résumé together, and to offering advice regarding the final draft.

By preparing your own résumé carefully and professionally you will find great satisfaction in the fact that you will have sold yourself. There are employers who view résumés prepared by professionals with suspicion. We have reviewed résumés prepared by "professionals" which border on "false advertising." There can be no question that professional placement offices and carefully selected professional résumé writers can be of great value for certain people. For example, high ranking managers or corporate executives who are necessarily burdened with major managerial functions or who require confidentiality may, of necessity, need to seek professional help. We urge that if at all possible, you prepare your own résumé: Do a complete, thorough analysis of your own life, and then, if necessary, consult with the professional. Do be certain that the final product is one that neither oversells nor undersells you; and that it meets your needs.

WRITING THE RÉSUMÉ

There are no panaceas or absolutes for writing the résumé. We can only hope to provide you with guidelines learned from our experiences and from those of successful applicants.

Some of the examples provided are long—some are too long. As a general rule a résumé should be short. Some interviewers state that one page is sufficient. We recommend that you include all necessary vital information but keep it as concise as you can—if this can be done in one page, fine; if more space is needed, take it, but use care.

In discussing the writing of the résumé, the authors have selected three basic résumés for analysis of content. The basic analysis will focus on the needs of the recent graduate with a few years experience seeking a change of careers, the more experienced manager/professional, and the person completing one long career and changing to another.

Choice of Materials

As with the letter of application, the choice of materials is important. As a minimum, the writer should use twenty pound, twenty-five per cent rag content paper in order to insure a good image. He should also be certain to type the résumé on a quality typewriter with an excellent ribbon, preferably a carbon ribbon. In addition, it may be helpful to have the letter of application and the résumé both typed on the same typewriter.

Since the writer may use several résumés in responding to a variety of possible positions, it may be desirable to have copies made. This is best accomplished by taking a crisp clean copy to a reputable printer and having it duplicated. This can be done by photo-offset, by lithographing, or by having it type-set. As of this writing, the cost will vary from $10.00 per hundred for copies made directly from your copy by offset or lithographic processing to $30.00 per hundred for type-set copies. Either method is acceptable; however, the type-set method offers the advantages of appearing more professional and of being condensed to fewer pages. For your comparison, most of the examples provided were photo-duplicated or lithographed while the final résumé (found in Appendix A) for Dr. Grattan was type-set. For the new graduate or applicant with minimal experience, the less expensive method is appropriate. Usually, it costs no more for one hundred copies than for ten, although the applicant should not require such a great number.

Under no condition should you ditto or mimeograph your résumé: The final copy appears purple, is of poor quality, and smears. Of course, there are some machines which do provide good quality black copies, and these are acceptable. We also recommend that you do not use a photocopy machine such as those found in department stores, since the copies are on a poor quality paper and tend to fade after a short period. The key is: Select the method which reflects the way *you* want the interviewer to *see* you.

Guidelines to Possible Content

TITLE

At the top of the first page, it is advisable to type the word: *RÉSUMÉ*. "Résumé" should be centered and double-spaced between the letters, as above. Such double-spacing is more esthetic since résumé is a short word. To be totally "correct," the word résumé has a diacritical marking called an acute accent (´) over each of the es since the word is French, and the accent marks indicate correct pronunciation. Since the word is rather common in English usage, there is a tendency to omit these markings; however, such a spelling is incorrect.

NAME AND PERSONAL DATA

As the reader can see in the accompanying examples, there are several ways one can handle any aspect of a résumé—the final choice is up to the applicant. In the Steven James Madison example (Figure 18) note that all personal data is provided at the top section of the first page. The advantage of this approach is that it requires an economy of space and provides the employer with all vital personal information at a glance. As a minimum, a résumé should include your complete name, complete address (both current and home addresses if more than one) with ZIP code, telephone number(s) and area code. In addition, it is

RESUME

STEVEN JAMES MADISON   Height: 6'2"
16 Durand Street   Weight: 195 lbs.
Miami, Florida 33140   Date of Birth: November 4, 1951
Telephone: 305-561-3173   Marital Status: Single

EDUCATION:
        1966-1970   Miami Senior High School,
                           Miami, Florida College Prepatory
                           Diploma 1970

        December 1973   B.S. (expected) State University of Florida,
                           College of Arts and Sciences,
                           Ft. Myers, Florida 33931
                           Major: Administrative Science/Economics
                           Specialization: Operation of Distribution
                             Channels

EMPLOYMENT:
        Summers of 1971, 1972 and 1973 Supermarkets General Corp.
                           Miami, Florida 33140
                           Nature of work: Inventory
                           Control Clerk

        Summer of 1970   Hendersons Bakery
                           Burlington, VT 06401
                           Nature of work: Production
                           Orientated

        Summer of 1969   City School District
                           Miami, Florida 33140
                           Nature of work: Painter

HONORS: Dean's List
          Readers Digest Scholarship Recipient
          Faculty Social Science Curriculum Committee
          Nominated for College Who's Who
          High School Sectional Football All-Star

EXTRA CURRICULAR ACTIVITIES & ORGANIZATIONS:

          President of Circle K Kiwanis Club - 1973
          Charter member of College Circle K Kiwanis Club - 1973
          President and Past Vice-President of the Administrative
            Science and Economic Organization 1970 - 1973
          Academic Affairs Board Treasurer of Student Association - 1973
          Finance Board member of Student Association - 1973
          Member of Florida State Varsity Football Team - 1970
          Photographer for College Newspaper - 1971 - 1973
          Pi Alpha Nu Fraternity 1972 - 1973

REFERENCES:
          Career Planning and Placement Office
          State University of Florida
          College of Arts and Sciences
          Ft. Myers, Florida 33931

Figure 18
Résumé by Steven James Madison

correct but not absolutely necessary to provide your height, weight, date of birth, and marital status. Obviously, if these items are to your advantage, include them. Perhaps if one were five feet tall and weighed two hundred and twenty pounds it would be preferable to let this statistic appear at the interview. The same is true for health situations such as *diabetes mellitus* or the loss of a limb. Other "problem" areas such as marital status and age are discussed in the final chapter, which will warrant your review. Remember, the purpose of the résumé is to help you to get the interview. Once there, you can "sell" yourself on your merits.

WHAT COMES NEXT?

At this point, we must interject that the data contained in a résumé is neither the same for all persons nor should it be considered in the same topical order. For a new graduate, it may be advisable to place your education as a top priority since your experience may be quite minimal. For the highly experienced manager, it may be desirable to place your experience first. For someone else who has specific goals or objectives, it may be desirable to place them first. The choice must be made after careful deliberation as to which will serve your purpose best. For the purpose of this chapter, we are considering the following order: professional objective, education, and then experience. This order is most common for the majority of applicants, especially younger ones.

PROFESSIONAL OBJECTIVE

There are several choices available to the applicant as to whether to use the term professional objective, personal goal, goal, or personal statement. Each would offer a similar purpose: to state clearly and concisely exactly what type of position you are seeking and what type of future you anticipate. Figure 19, the Phillips example, provides an excellent statement of an objective:

RESUME

Everett L. Phillips   Height: 5'9"
65 Leonard Avenue   Weight: 165 lbs.
Plattsburgh, New York 12901   Birthdate: August 2, 1943
Telephone: (518) 561-3333   Married: Wife, Elizabeth
                                          Son, Scott (4 mos.)

Professional
Objective   A responsible and challenging position which utilizes a background
                   in business management, economics and electronic data processing,
                   with opportunity for future advancement. Particularly interested
                   in all phases of data processing and/or opportunities in management.

Education   CENTRAL KENTUCKY UNIVERSITY, LOUISVILLE, KENTUCKY, 60610. B.S.
Formal   in Business Administration, 1966. MAJOR: Business Management,
                   with special emphasis on data processing, accounting and economics.

Technical   U.S. AIR FORCE MANAGEMENT ANALYSIS OFFICER COURSE, Wichita Falls,
                   Texas. 100 hour course in statistical analysis, data presentation,
                   program and financial analysis and personnel management techniques.
                   Completed July 1967.

                   U.S. AIR FORCE OFFICER TRAINING SCHOOL, San Antonio, Texas. 90
                   day intensive training course in military leadership, personnel
                   management techniques and written and oral communication tech-
                   niques. Upon completion in May 1967, received a commission as
                   an officer in the U.S. Air Force.

Experience   STATE UNIVERSITY COLLEGE OF ARTS AND SCIENCE, Plattsburgh, New York.
June 1971   Programmer-Analyst: Employed in the Office of Records, Analytical
to   Studies and Long Range Planning with primary duties as Coordinator
Present   of Registration. Responsible for hiring, training, supervising
                   and evaluating employees utilized during Registration activities.
                   Also responsible for planning, implementing, supervising and
                   follow-up of all functions and facets of the Registration system.
                   Provides interface between programmers and data processing per-
                   sonnel, the Registrar's Office and the Office of Analytical Studies
                   in order to update and perfect the Registration system. Utilizes
                   analytical capabilities to assess the accuracy, speed and success
                   of Registration procedures. Produces analytical data necessary
                   to complete reports and maintain information files.

Feb. 1967   UNITED STATES AIR FORCE, Plattsburgh, New York.
to   Management Analysis Officer (CAPTAIN): Responsible for training,
May 1971   supervising and evaluating approximately six civilian and military
                   personnel. Served as acting Comptroller in the absence of the
                   Base Comptroller. Specialized in the preparation and presentation
                   of oral briefings, statistical digests and management aids to key
                   personnel and staff. Responsible for the preparation and presen-
                   tation of management studies and statistical analyses intended to
                   identify specific trends or problem areas. Recommendations and

Figure 19
Résumé by Everett L. Phillips

solutions proposed in these studies resulted in improved management procedures and cost savings. Utilized computer products to perform cost analysis function of base cost centers.

Mar. 1966
to
Feb. 1967

GENERAL MOTORS AUDITING DIVISION, Flint, Michigan.
Data Processing and Management Trainee: As a participant in the College Graduate in Training Program, received training and experience in all facets of the data processing operation. Also, received training in management procedures and operation of all the departments in the central office of General Motros Parts Division. Worked on special projects in the Electronic Data Processing Quality Control Section.

June 1966
to
Sept. 1966

MICHIGAN POWER COMPANY, Grand Rapids, Michigan
Assistant Gas Supply Supervisor in the Gas Telemetering Department. Responsible for dispatching and metering the natural gas flow throughout the Michigan Power Company system. Duties included responsibility for approximately $700,000 worth of telemetering equipment and facilities.

Summers of
1962, '63
and '64

DIVISION STEEL AND ALLOY SUPPLY COMPANY, Grand Rapids, Michigan
General Office and Clerical Duties: Experience included the computation and validation of semi-annual inventory levels, in addition to performing general clerical duties.

Background

Born and educated in Louisville, Kentucky. Member of the National Honor Society. Junior and Senior Class Vice-President. 4 years of varsity baseball (high school). Participated in college intramural sports. Sigma Pi Social fraternity. Member of the Central Kentucky University Consultative Council on Administration. Earned approximately 30% of college expenses through summer jobs and part-time work.

Personal
Interests

Hobbies include skiing, tennis, bicycling, golf and hiking. Am also interested in service organizations and community service. Member of Rotary International.

References

References are available upon request.

Figure 19 (continued)

A responsible and challenging position which utilizes a background in business management, economics and electronic data processing, with opportunity for future advancement. Particularly interested in all phases of data processing and/or opportunities in management.

This statement concisely incorporates elements from Mr. Phillips' background, his area of immediate interest, and his long range objective—future advancement. Figure 20 is rather similar although it provides a brief, chronological progression of Mr. Trombley's career which reaches a climax in stating his goal as ". . . a senior position in sales management in Southwest U.S." We do not recommend limiting yourself to one area of the country or, especially, to one city unless this is an absolute must with you. In today's society the work force is highly mobile, with numerous managers and professionals moving freely from one state to another. It is quite wise to orient yourself and your family to anticipate a move and to make such a venture an exciting, enjoyable one.

You will note that Figure 18, by Mr. Madison, does not give a goal.[2] For a majority of younger prospective employees this may not be necessary since you may need to be available for a wide range of options. However, the letter of application should then provide such data. There is the danger that, in limiting one's goal too much, one narrows one's options, thus missing some excellent opportunities. If you do elect to state your professional objective, be certain that it is compatible with the education and work experiences delineated within your résumé.

EDUCATION

There can be no question that an applicant having a high

[2]Figures 18 and 19 represent experimental résumés designed to test the effectiveness of the format. Mr. Madison interviewed for seven openings at a college placement office. Six of the seven interviewers offered him a position. Mr. Phillips, a well known acquaintance of the authors, agreed to participate in a broad experiment. His final résumé was mailed to fifty-nine companies in 1974. Fifty-four responded within two weeks. Twenty responses either requested additional information or asked that the applicant come for an interview. The applicant narrowed the list to five; interviewed with the company of his first choice; and obtained the position.

R E S U M E

George F. Trombley   Date of Birth: May 6, 1933
55 Draper Avenue   Height: 5'11"
Ann Arbor, Michigan 48112   Weight: 190 lbs.
Phone: 313-656-3324   Health: Excellent

OBJECTIVE: Following a career which began as a helper in a greenhouse,
expanding to a partnership in a million dollar plus enterprise,
and, finally, to a major interest in horticultural plastic sales,
desire a senior position in sales management in Southwest U. S.

EXPERIENCE SUMMARY: After graduating from high school served from 1951 to
1957 as a soil mixer, planter, plant propagator, salesman, and
delivery man for Mason's Greenhouse, Ann Arbor, Michigan. Due
to excellent growth and sales potential, was offered a 49%
share of the organization. From 1957 until 1965 increased
commercial flower sales from $75,000 per year to over $1,000,000
per year. Full partnership fulfilled in 1965. From 1965 until
1970 continued to expand operation to include a major artificial
soils division. In 1970, again expanded operation to include a
franchise with International Plastics for all horticultural
plastics for the State. Due to the retirement of my partner
and to the extensive growth of the corporation, desire to sell
and to focus my talents within the area of sales management.

SALES EXPERIENCE: Extensive experience ranging from direct sales to
mail order operations to bulk commercial sales. Have had
seven consecutive years personal sales in excess of $1,000,000.
Am also familiar with advertising layout and design, pricing,
and distribution.

MANAGEMENT/SUPERVISION: As vice-president have been totally responsible for hiring, training, and supervision of all personnel.
Presently, have in excess of thirty employees on location and
a similar number in the field. Total sales exceed $3,000,000.
Am also responsible for all planning, expansion, development
and research, accounting, payrolls, budgeting, equipment,
building and grounds. Also represent corporation at national
and state conventions.

PROFESSIONAL ORGANIZATIONS: Member of the American Horticulture Association, Michigan Growers Association, the American Management
Association, and the United States Plastics Association.

PERSONAL INTERESTS: Am nationally recognized expert in propagation of
roses. Also active in community affairs and am a member of
the Junior Chamber of Commerce, Rotary International, and a
member of the Hospital Board.

REFERENCES: Highest references available upon request.

Figure 20
Résumé of George F. Trombley

school diploma, an advanced degree, or other advanced education may want to include it in his résumé. Logically, the younger a person is the more important his education becomes. In fact, it may well be the determining factor that helps him to land his first position. For the highly experienced technician or manager, education may be of a lower priority than his proven experience; thus experience should be given higher priority. In Figure 18, Mr. Madison has an excellent educational background but rather limited experience. Thus we would recommend that he place his education first. With Mr. Phillips in Figure 19, there is a choice: His education and experience are both significant; yet one does not outweigh the other. In such a case, we would recommend placing education first since his employment record would probably continue to the second sheet anyway. In Figure 20, it is obvious that Mr. Trombley's education is quite secondary to his proven record of accomplishment.

Regardless of the style used in writing your résumé, if you are an experienced manager, a professional, or a highly experienced person changing careers, and if you have significant education, integrate that information into your résumé with some degree of primacy.

Numerous persons with years of experience have attended a wide variety of additional schools, correspondence courses, workshops, or seminars. Figure 19 demonstrates a useful method of listing such schools. Note that Mr. Phillips did not simply attend a U.S. Air Force Management Analysis Officer Course in Wichita Falls, Texas. He attended a "100 hour course in statistical analysis, data presentation. . . ." Such a brief description is much more beneficial than a meaningless generalization. For members of the military who have attended several schools, we recommend that you select those schools and courses which are related to the civilian career you intend to pursue and be certain to write the description in terms of that civilian position— avoid military numbers and jargon. Members of the military should also be alerted to the fact that numerous military courses are not only capable of being equated with civilian positions but have been evaluated for a significant number of college, vocational or academic credits. For this information, see a Base

Education Officer or Counselor and ask that your military training be evaluated. For all branches of the Armed Forces, the American Council on Education has edited a *Guide To The Evaluation of Educational Experiences in the Armed Services* which gives a delineation of all military courses along with any academic credit evaluation.[3] In addition, there are other sources of military coursework and credits, such as that provided in the catalogue of the Community College of the Air Force.[4]

We have found a wide variety of sources for educational experiences, such as the American Management Association, Civil Service Courses, Police Academies, the American Banking Institute, and extension courses provided by high schools and colleges. The point is: Although we urge that you be selective and sell yourself, we do suggest that you consider including important educational opportunities which you might overlook. Sometimes, it can be helpful to illustrate personal and professional growth by demonstrating your continuing education.

Educators. For applicants within the field of education, it is usually necessary to list all education from secondary school to the present. Since you have selected a career within education, a primary concern is whether you have the academic credentials necessary. Prior to an interview you may even be requested to forward copies of your transcripts.

Guidelines. As a rule, list college degrees and any other relevant education or training. Use such information only if it helps to make you more attractive—marketable. In writing this information avoid initials, since numerous schools or courses

[3]*Guide To The Evaluation of Educational Experiences in the Armed Services,* 1974 Edition, edited by Jerry W. Miller and Eugene J. Sullivan for the Commission on Educational Credit of the American Council on Education, a non-copyrighted work in the interest of education, available from the American Council on Education, One Dupont Circle, Washington, D.C. 20036. Service personnel should consult their Base Education Office for this Guide.

[4]*General Catalog, 1974-75,* of the Community College of the Air Force. The Community College of the Air Force is an accredited institution which provides evaluations and transcripts of military courses for vocational credits. This is a useful service for all Air Force personnel with vocational training programs. Consult your Base Education Officer for proper forms.

have the same initials. Be certain to make any description provided meaningful to the person who is to read your résumé.

EXPERIENCE

There is probably no more important part of your résumé than the selection and presentation of your experience. For managerial, administrative, or advanced technical or research fields, an excellent "picture" of your work experience will do more to get you "that" position than any other item. In presenting your experience, begin with your most recent experience and work in inverse chronological order. It is important that you concentrate upon descriptions which will convince the employer that you fill the bill.

If you are seeking a managerial position, there are at least three important dimensions you might consider. A manager must be a leader. In this respect, show your experiences with *human resources*—show that you can work with people and motivate them to excel. In Figure 19 by Phillips, we read: " . . . Responsible for hiring, training, supervising and evaluating employees. . . ." In Figure 20 by Trombley, ". . . have in excess of thirty employees on location and a similar number in the field. Total sales exceed $3,000,000. . . ." Other data might include experience in training, development of personal programs, work with collective negotiations, affirmative action, minorities, or incentive programs. Examine the résumés provided (in Appendix A) to see how various applicants handled their experience with human resources.

A second consideration is your experience with *material resources*. Here you might discuss work objectives in terms of accomplishments in dollars earned or saved, budget experience, new innovations, outstanding programs with results specified, or other significant monetary experience. In Mr. Phillips' experience with the Michigan Power Company he states: "Duties included responsibility for approximately $700,000 worth of telemetering equipment and facilities." In a later résumé by Mr. Douglas (See Appendix A), who is seeking a senior pilot/management position, we read: "Responsibilities include supervision of seventy-eight civilian and military personnel. Responsible for all aspects of ground training and budgeting. Managing the utilization and maintenance of $35 million worth of Training Devices with an annual supply budget of $93 thousand." Can you produce materially? If so, document it with sufficient specifics.

Finally, what are your significant *personal resources?* What can *you* do? Mr. Trombley in Figure 20 grew from a helper to a major partner capable of personal sales in excess of $1,000,000. In addition he is capable of considerable growth potential— actually, he is quite a go-getter. If your major responsibilities are "marketable," spell them out. Persons in education may wish to review Dr. Grattan's résumé, included among the examples in Appendix A.

DISPLAYING YOUR WORK EXPERIENCE

After considering your experience in terms of human, material, and personal resources, there are at least three basic ways in which you can compose your experiences: chronologically, functionally, or "strategically."

Chronological Listing. In using this display method, you should list all of your positions in reverse order, with your most recent work experience first. In surveying numerous résumés, this appears to be the most common method used and it has proven successful. This method is used almost exclusively by persons seeking positions in teaching or nursing. Logically, this method provides you with the opportunity to show the maturation you have gained in experience over the years. Additional résumés for study are provided in Appendix A. Some of these résumés, such as Russell's and Grattan's, offer an excellent overview of personal growth. Others, such as Nelson's and Castle's, are too repetitious and long. Redundancy and the inclusion of experience which no longer interest you are potential weaknesses.

Functional Listing. Although Figure 20 by Mr. Trombley is not necessarily the best example of this method, note his listing of a brief summary, his sales experience, and then his management/supervision experience. An applicant in sales might list his sales capabilities and potential, his experience with management, marketing, or distribution. An educator seeking an administrative position might include experience in teaching, special activities, positions of leadership, scholarship, research, or experience in areas such as fund raising, budgeting, or student affairs. A high school student might even use this method in a limited fashion by depicting his experience—limited as it must be—in a manner that will demonstrate his potential. For example: "My limited experience as a waitress has provided me with the opportunity to establish myself as a responsible, reliable employee, and has given me the opportunity to develop excellent communicative skills. I consider my ability to meet the public and to carry out my responsibilities with ease to be major assets. My significant earnings in tips substantiates my abilities."

Strategical Listing. A debate coach teaches his students to state a major issue, to support it with sufficient valid evidence, and to reach a conclusion. An applicant using this approach is encouraged to state the specific goal or type of position desired; and to document it with relevant, specific data about his education or experience in order to prove his potential to meet the responsibilities of the position. He should be certain that the data are clear, specific, and sufficient for the employer to reach the logical conclusion that he is needed by the company.

PERSONAL DATA

Personal data take many forms, such as statistics about yourself, your personal interests, community service, and honors or awards. Some experts believe that most of this data should be left for the interview. Although the choice must be yours and must be considered with care, we recommend that significant data of this type can aid you to get the interview and can be used with discretion to demonstrate your attributes. Such data can also provide the interviewer with ideas for questions that will enable him to learn more about your abilities and interests. Our research has revealed that the majority of interviewers are NOT professional, experienced interviewers and that they do not enjoy this task. Thus, anything that you can do to help them to be comfortable and to carry out this task with confidence can be in your favor. Large companies will, as a rule, have well-trained, highly qualified interviewers. Even then, you will find that they are human and have their "moments"—days when they are inspired and days when they wish they had stayed in bed. It's your task to be able to back up your résumé with the outstanding person it is supposed to reflect. Review the résumés provided in this chapter and in Appendix A with care. Although each writer did find his résumé successful, the same may not be true in your case with the same approach.

REFERENCES

Under most conditions, you should not include your references. Think of yourself as the employer. Would you not have a tendency to view such references with suspicion? An applicant will not provide references which he feels would be unfavorable. Now, view yourself as one of the references. Suppose several employers called—what would be the quality of your third, fifth, or eighth response? We recommend that you select references who can honestly and fully describe your assets and that you have such a list ready when asked to provide it. If you are a recent college graduate or a person who has a current placement folder, then you can list this information; however, do state that "Placement credentials are available upon request or from. . . ." Show a personal willingness to provide either your credentials or additional references. Should an advertisement require references, you should provide them.

Having written your résumé, proofread against these guidelines:

1. Does the finished document reflect positively on me? Why wear a suit and tie or an attractive dress, if your résumé looks as if it had been prepared by a second or third-rate writer?

2. Is the résumé short and in correct English? Is it written in the active voice—subject, verb, predicate? The active voice reads quickly and sells.

3. Is the résumé free of errors? Proofread and then proofread again. Perhaps the best way to proofread is to read aloud. Be certain to have a competent person read your résumé. Often, he will be able to spot errors or weaknesses better than you can. A spouse or close friend will also be able to identify any significant omissions you may have made. If you are in doubt about spelling or anything else—LOOK IT UP!

4. Although you may have duplicate copies of your résumé reproduced, do not mass produce your letter of application. An employer looks upon form letters as most of us do upon "junk" mail. Duplicated letters show little initiative.

5. If you have used the services of a printer, did you proofread the final copy carefully to include every comma and punctuation mark? The final copy is your responsibility. If your letter and résumé are typed, have you made an effort to have the quality of the paper and the typing match? This is also advisable, if the multilith company has provided numerous copies of your résumé from your original.

6. Is the résumé current? Any applicant who uses an outdated résumé is either careless or not a serious applicant.

7. Did you prepare the envelope with the same care as your résumé and letter? Full names and address? Correct spelling? Did you have the letter weighed for correct postage? Did you apply the postage?

If you are satisfied that you can prepare both your letter of application and your résumé with care, you are now ready to review the following check list and the sample résumés in Appendix A; and then to look at the chapters on interviewing and potential concerns you may encounter.

CHECK LIST OF POTENTIAL AREAS
FOR INCLUSION IN A *RÉSUMÉ*

A résumé is a brief profile of oneself which is made available to a potential employer prior to an interview. As such, it is an unsolicited advertisement which provides the employer with a review of one's background and potential. This check list provides a summary of numerous items which one might include in a résumé. Obviously, each applicant should select only those which relate to him. The list is not all inclusive; so be certain to consider any strengths or areas which might be omitted. A review of these items will provide you with areas for thought as you review this chapter.

Résumé of	Provide your name in full. You may want to place it at the top of each page.
Current Address	Be certain your current address is complete, is spelled correctly, and includes your ZIP code. Also include your telephone number and area code.
Permanent Address	Provide your permanent address if different from your current address—include your address and telephone number with the area code.
Goals and/or Objectives	*If* this is applicable to your specific résumé then prepare it carefully in advance.
Position or Job Title	You should include your present position or title. Be concise and specific, such as: Assistant Buyer for Blaine's Men's Clothing.
Educational Record	Include your secondary school, post secondary school work, dates of graduation, certification,

professional schools, civil service schools, military schools. Do list all college degrees and your major and minor areas of study.

Employment Record

Maintain a list of all previous employment; however, you may select your most recent years of employment. Some employers want a comprehensive delineation of all employment. Try to illustrate how your work is compatible with the position being sought. Usually, you should begin with your latest position and work back chronologically. Include the beginning and ending dates of each position.

Military Employment (Career)

Members of the military who have spent several years encompassing several bases may find it useful to summarize their experience. In many cases this may be broken to include: latest position, which is usually the most significant and of a managerial nature; the middle years of your career, which may be technical in nature; and the beginning of your career, which probably included initial schools and basic positions. If you have cross-trained, then this would need to be included.

Military Status

For those applicants who are not career persons, be brief and to the point regarding your experiences or classification.

Activities/Interests

These should be selected to suit your level. A high school graduate might include positions of leadership in school organizations or his extra curricular activities, while one with several years of experience would prefer to include community work, professional organizations, offices, or other personal interests. List only relevant activities or interests which will provide meaningful insights into what type of person you may be.

Published Works

Do include all published works—unless too prolific—then, be selective.

Professional Organizations

Do include all (with offices held), since these illustrate a breadth of activity and involvement.

Licenses and Certificates

If relevant, be certain to include these.

Mastery of Languages

For many positions, the mastery of a second language can be a major asset.

An Unusual Asset

Some applicants have a significant skill which might not be apparent unless specifically identified.

Personal Data

Should include date of birth, height, weight, marital status (even name of wife/husband may be useful), health (see Chapter 6, Special Problems).

References

You should have a list of references to be made available; but do not include them in your résumé. Provide the address of any Placement Office having your records.

CHAPTER THREE

Preparing for the Interview

Recently we spoke with numerous people involved in the process of job interviewing. Among them were managers and supervisors. Some worked in personnel offices. Others included tradespeople helping to select their future co-workers. All with whom we talked had years of experience in their fields, either in providing numerous employment recommendations or in the actual hiring of new employees. One common complaint about applicants emerged again and again—*NOT* that the applicant lacked experience or training; but that he showed a "lack of interest and enthusiasm both in the interview being conducted and in the job being discussed." Despite the desire of the candidates and the obvious importance of the interview, applicants persistently communicated the opposite impression: "I'm really *not* very interested and really don't care."

One large company vice president describes the problem this way: "Interviewers are continually amazed at the number of applicants who drift into job interviews without any apparent preparation and only the vaguest idea of what they are going to say. Their manner says, 'Well, here we are', and that's often the end of it, in more ways than one."

Impressions of boredom, of disinterest, inattention, or apathy may be created by many causes ranging from a fear of being interviewed to simply not knowing what to expect. Whatever the cause, such a negative impact must be avoided; it must be replaced by a more positive and enthusiastic posture. Confidence and competence are learned. Successful interviews result from better understanding and preparation.

WHAT IS AN EMPLOYMENT INTERVIEW?

An employment interview is a *conversation* between two or more persons. You may feel it is more formal than most of your conversations. However, you should approach the interview as though it were an important conversation with someone who can help you in your career. Thinking of the interview as a serious conversation with a helpful friend may help you to develop that "positive" attitude.

Think of the interview as a *preplanned conversation* with a *structure* and a *purpose*. Usually the employer, or his representative, will open and close that phase of the interview in which the main line of questions and discussion take place. This does not necessarily mean that the interviewer should or must always take the lead in structuring the interview. It does mean that this is one of the interviewer's primary tasks in the question-answer sequence. Your role is to be alert, to be patient, to listen, and to react. Above all you must be an *active* participant.

WHAT'S IT ALL ABOUT?

The purposes of employment interviews differ in both type and degree. Generally, they are both *information-giving* and *information-seeking*. In this sense they are informational conversations in which the interviewer seeks information from you, the job applicant; but they are also times at which you, the applicant, seek information from the interviewer. The balance in the dialogue need not be 50-50. In a brief interview, or when the interviewer is inexperienced, you may find him doing nearly all of the talking.

Ideally, there should be a balance *between* the participants so that each both gives and gets information. What should be emphasized here is that the employment interview is an opportunity for the job applicant to learn additional information about the job, its characteristics and work conditions; about the employees; about supervision and management; and about the company and its policies. Think of your role as that of an information seeker and you will soon find yourself a more active and eager participant. Be sincere, concerned, and openly interested with finding out about *this* company and *this* position. There are so many things for you to learn through the interview if you can develop a spirit of "sharing information" with the interviewer—sharing perceptions about the company, about the job, about the employees, about the community.

Another informational purpose is finding out about the possibilities for "making a deal." Sometimes the job should be filled immediately and at other times it is more remote. Just as applicants are sometimes more immediately available, or desperate, they are sometimes not ready to come to terms. Often, at initial employment interviews, the topic of terms and conditions of employment is not even discussed; while other interviews are devoted almost entirely to a discussion of these subjects. Here again, we do not have a 50-50 situation. One participant may strongly seek information on a topic while another may avoid the topic altogether, change the subject, and provide information on a completely different bent. Frequent advice given job applicants on topics such as salary is to let the interviewer take the lead. You might inquire in a general way, but do not push or probe prematurely. Patience and poise reflect maturity and confidence.

In addition to the informative purposes of employment interviews, there are at least two persuasive purposes. Interviewers frequently use the employment interview as an opportunity to sell you on their company (whether or not they intend to hire you at this time). Their purpose, a legitimate one for this type of interview, is to convince you that this is an excellent position with an outstanding firm.

What you should not overlook is the opportunity that the

employment interview provides you. This is your chance to convince and to persuade, too. This is your opportunity to convince the employer that you are the best candidate for the job. Once again, this is your invitation to be an active, interested, and enthusiastic participant. It is your opportunity to be persuasive in helping the interviewer form positive or favorable impressions of you.

In a study conducted by Northwestern University's Graduate School of Business, questionnaires and interviews were conducted with 76 professional college recruiters and large numbers of job candidates. One important question asked related to the purpose of the employment interview. That question was: "What is the primary objective of the interview?" The overwhelming first choice answer was: "To find out what kind of person the candidate is." Overall, 78 percent of the professional interviewers and 68 percent of the candidates indicated that "finding out what kind of person the candidate is" was the primary objective of the selection interviewer. Interviewers and candidates alike ranked that question as more important than "providing information about the job" or "determining a candidate's non-personal qualifications."[1]

Of utmost importance to employers is the concern over whether "they can get along" with the person they hire. "Can we live with him on the job?" is the big question on the interviewer's mind.

If we are going to be convincing to employers, we must discover those personal qualities of cooperation, pleasantness, and compatability in ourselves that will appeal to interviewers. We must then sell those qualities in us by finding ways to reveal and to communicate them to interviewers. That is our purpose in the employment interview.

---

[1]See article by Calvin W. Downs, "What Does the Selection Interview Accomplish?" in *Readings in Interpersonal and Organizational Communication,* ed. R. C. Huesman, D. L. Freshley and C. M. Logue (Boston: Holbrook Press, 1969), pp. 287-88.

WHAT ARE THE TYPES OF
EMPLOYMENT INTERVIEWS?

There are two types of employment interviews you will want to distinguish in order to avoid confusion and possible disappointment. Some companies begin their search for eligible candidates with a screening interview. The *screening interview,* unlike the final *selection interview,* is often quite brief and is designed so that a number of candidates can be met on a personal basis and quickly classified as either qualified or not qualified, as either suitable or not suitable for the position.

Screening interviews are often quite narrow, in that they center around just a few of the most essential qualifications being sought in the position. Recently, a senior college student explained how disappointed she was with her job interview. "It was so short," she complained, "I didn't have a chance to ask many questions, and we didn't cover very much at all, and I don't know if I ever want to go through that again. I'm pretty disgusted about the whole thing."

What this frustrated student failed to realize was that she had experienced only an initial screening interview, and that because of its nature there was little opportunity to cover the broad range of topics she wanted to discuss in depth. Initial screening interviews seldom allow for such exploration and are often limited to only five or ten minutes. Fortunately, the student was called again for a subsequent interview, in which she had the opportunity to discuss the things she had hoped to pursue.

Do not be startled to find yourself in another type of interview—the *multi-participant interview.* Frequently, a job applicant is called on to be interviewed simultaneously by the boss or manager and a supervisor, or by a selection committee. This type of group interview situation, with two or more interviewers asking questions, perhaps on different topics (or trains of thought), can be hectic for an interviewee. You must try to maintain your poise and composure by concentrating on just one question at a time. By calmly giving your full attention and concentration first to one interviewer's question and then to the other's (while politely acknowledging interruptions with a nod or a smile), you will force the interviewers into waiting their respective turns and perhaps even into listening to your answering the other person's questions.

This is the calm and confident approach one must take to the group interview as well as to the *selection committee interview.* Because of the demands on employers to be "Equal Opportunity Employers" and because of the laws and standards upheld by the Equal Employment Opportunity Commission, employers now find it necessary to advertise widely and to recruit actively for applicants from minority groups. Because of the immense volume of work this creates, selection committees are often formed to work closely with the company's affirmative action officer. One can anticipate a selection committee interview in such situations where the decision to hire is influenced by the recommendations of a panel or committee selected to review all of the final candidates (those not eliminated from the large numbers of applicants).

Occasionally, you may encounter a type of interview known by its stress or pressure approach. Instead of putting you at ease, the interviewer may attempt to get you emotionally aroused.

"I want to see how the individual handles himself under pressure and stress," an adjustment house (collection agency) employer recently told us. "The people who work for me," this general manager went on, "must be able to face people who are angry about their bills. They'll face every type of excuse and con in the book. Are they going to be afraid to speak up? Can they be firm in the face of anger and hostility or will they wilt under pressure?"

To discover how "the individual handles himself," this manager admitted to "giving job applicants a hard time." He deliberately began the interview with bluntness and sometimes sarcasm to see if the applicant would become unnerved.

Although this pressure-approach type interview is not too common, the stress interview is occasionally used by industrial interviewers. Like the adjustment house manager, these interviewers are convinced that the ability to handle many types of stress on the job is vital to success. They believe that an applicant's ability to adjust to a wide variety of people, including the aggressive, the disturbed, and the upset, can be detected during the pressure of the interview.

Some of the unusual contrivances of these interviewers include: staring, introducing deliberate interruptions and distractions, changing the pace of the interview, creating long uncomfortable pauses, and being overly critical, blunt, harsh, or offensive.

Learning to adjust and maintain control and poise during such unusual circumstances in the interview is critical to being selected for such a job.

Another unusual form of group interview was called to our attention recently when a young teacher asked what she could do in the following interview situation. A representative from the education ministry of a foreign country was scheduled to arrive on campus to interview teachers for positions abroad. The young applicant knew that the representative would call together in one room the nine final candidates being considered for teaching abroad. She knew from the placement office director that the representative would begin by explaining the nature of the three positions available and would then answer questions about them.

However, following that phase of the meeting, the representative was scheduled to continue his interviewing—not by interviewing one candidate at a time but by interviewing all applicants at the *same* time.

"What shall I do?" she asked. "How can one make a favorable impression in a group scene like that?"

The "eclectic" strategy recommended and discussed in this *multi*-interviewee situation resulted in the following scenario:

"After the representative finishes his briefing and begins answering questions from the group," the professor advised, "you can anticipate that several candidates will seize the opportunity to speak up quickly. But wait! Don't be too anxious. Be patient and listen as attentively as you can. When your turn does come, demonstrate some of the qualities of a good teacher.''

Well, she went to that interview and sure enough, no sooner had the interviewer finished his question, than several respondents pushed forward with ready answers. Each candidate seized every opportunity to break into the dialogue and speak up quickly. It looked as though every candidate was vying for the quickest and best answer. The interpersonal competition was on, with one exception. Our young teacher, as coached, simply waited, kept her composure, and listened. She listened well and said nothing for a long while. Finally, the interviewer called on her for her interpretation of a difficult question, noting as he did so that she had not yet spoken.

"Well," she replied, "I've been quiet because I've been listening to the others here. Now I agree with part of what Bob said when he explained . . . . I believe Bill made a good point when he said that . . . . About the only thing that I want to add is. . . ."

By listening so well that she could directly repeat each participant's best point, unify each contribution into a thorough response, and add a significant personal point to the whole of it, our teacher made a very favorable impression. In that one answer, she demonstrated the qualities of good concentration, good listening comprehension, and the ability to adapt to others and to the situation quickly. The interviewing skills of listening through a question, summarizing, and respecting everyone's contributions apply to all interviews.

We don't know if this technique will ever help get you a job, but we do know that it helped our young teacher in a most unique group interview situation.

WHAT ARE THE STEPS IN PREPARATION?

You have now viewed the employment interview from the perspective of purpose and opportunity. It should be your purpose to get information and to persuade through the interview.

You have also seen a few of the different types of employment interviews. To add more to your understanding, let us move on to the big question: How do I prepare?

Step 1: Personal Inventory: Take Stock of Yourself

The first step in preparing for the employment interview begins by analyzing *you*. You need to begin by taking stock of yourself. Your personal inventory should explore the common characteristics between you and your career plans.

The philosophic dictum "Know thyself" advises us to begin with the question, "Who Am I?" Who am I, in terms of my personal goals, and in terms of my professional goals? Do I work best in the company of others or when alone? Do I prefer outdoor or indoor work? Am I willing to travel constantly, occasionally, or only infrequently? Would being away from my family for various periods of time be an important factor in my accepting or rejecting a certain type of job? Would I be opposed to working solely on a commission basis? What salary range would I be willing to work in without constantly worrying about money? Would I be comfortable speaking publicly to large and small groups? Could I represent the company before large audiences? Would I be willing to relocate in another state? Would I be willing to begin in a one year training program at half salary in order to improve my skills and competencies?

Two distinct categories of questions and resulting information emerge through this type of self-inspection. There are, on the one hand, considerations of your personal needs and goals. Needs and goals stem either from the position in which you live or from the ambitions and desires you hope to attain. On the other hand, there are your interests and attitudes, which form another body of information about you. Happy is the person whose interests and attitudes correspond with his goals and needs. This is frequently not the case. A person may, for instance, be interested in working in the outdoors. His attitudes might favor his being a "loner" and doing manual labor. His health and financial needs, however, may not allow him to engage in the luxury of satisfying those interests and attitudes to the extent he would prefer.

Take the case of Bill, a young college student who was heard to say that he was interested in getting a job on a farm or as a forester because he loved the out-of-doors and he didn't enjoy working inside an office, a building, or a truck or car.

The truth of the matter was that the young man's acute asthma prevented him from working in the out-of-doors during several weeks of the year. He often needed an air-conditioned room. And his financial obligations wouldn't permit him to consider accepting one of the low-paying, farm-hand positions that was available.

One needs to look realistically at oneself and find a balance between one's interests and one's needs, between one's attitude and one's goals. Two additional areas of concern in this analysis are one's knowledge and skills in relation to one's health and physical ability.

Although one might be knowledgeable and skillful in, for instance, masonry work, one may not have the physical stamina or good health to perform such tasks on a regular on-the-job, full-time schedule or basis.

You need to ask yourself, honestly, questions such as the following:

A. Regarding my knowledge and skills, in which fields do I have the greatest background, practical experience, or job skills? For what has my training best prepared me? In what areas do I have more talent, natural ability, or job skills than most other people?

B. Regarding my health and general physical ability, how long can I work on my feet before I have to sit down and rest? Do I have difficulty going up and down stairs, lifting heavy objects, or driving a car or truck for long periods at a stretch? Would certain types of work create eye strain or headaches? How physically tolerant could I be regarding shop noise, odors, various temperatures, or other working conditions? For what types of activities do I have the greatest stamina—for what types the least?

For a complete set of inventory questions under these four categories, see the Personal Inventory Checklist (Table 1) at the end of Chapter Four. The information from these four areas (see Figure 21) should provide you with a better sighting, a more accurate aim toward your personal career potential.

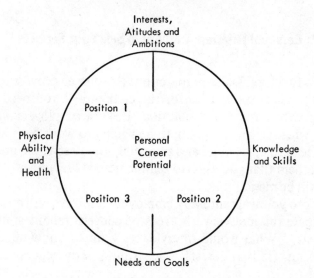

Because you (1) *consider your personal and professional needs and goals,* you are likely to see where they are in agreement or in conflict. You are more likely to *set new goals.* You are likely to narrow down your specific occupational choices.

Because you (2) *consider your interests and attitudes,* you are more likely to find career choices that will increase your interests and appetites for professional growth.

Because you (3) *survey your past experience, education, and training,* you will seek careers that can build upon your expertise, feelings of confidence, and self-worth.

Because you (4) *consider your physical stamina and general health,* you are more likely to avoid being over-extended, inundated, or boxed into the wrong type of job.

Perhaps this first step might be summarized with an analogy. Imagine that you are looking down the scope of a rifle. Your task is to sight it in on the target for a perfect bull's eye. The cross hairs of your scope are the extensions of the considerations just discussed. You will have to make allowances and adjustments for your shortcomings just as a rifleman makes allowances for wind drift and distance. Can you align your sights on the most suitable target as illustrated in Figure 21?

Step 2: Personal Briefing: Prepare to Sell Your Services

Step two is self-sales preparation. Because employers want to know "What can you do for the company?" you need to be prepared to answer that question. Because employers want to know whether you are going to be willing to work hard, and to be dependable, reliable, and punctual, you need to be prepared to tell them that you are—to tell them and show them in a way that will be memorable.

Before you walk into any employment interview, you should anticipate the interviewer's areas of concern (about you). Ask yourself, "What would interviewers want to know about me, about my skills, interests, background, experiences, or attitudes?"

We are not advocating that you should have a canned or pat answer for all of these questions. We are suggesting that you should have thought them through. As implied in Step one, you should both "get your facts straight" and prepare to present them descriptively. Herein is the distinction between preparing your thoughts and memorizing a line.

For example, a most common question is "What experiences have you had in connection with this type of work?" If you have failed to take stock of yourself and failed to think through your input into the interview, you will not be prepared to avoid vague and inept answers, such as: "Oh, I don't really know" or "I'm not sure" or "I've had some but not really too much." Such answers do not provide much information. They do not help the interviewer with his problem of validity, nor do they help him to obtain accurate and reliable data about you. Most importantly, such responses do not convince or persuade.

If your hasty answer is a blustery, "Oh, I've had lots and lots of experience of many types in this line of work," the interviewer will most likely want to follow up with probing questions. "Where did you acquire this experience? What did you learn from it? When did this occur? Among your past employers who could best speak of your past experiences? How long did you work there?"

Failure to reply to such follow-up questions will quickly expose your first answer (about having had "lots and lots of experience") as a gross generalization. What's worse, you are likely to be perceived as a phony, as a braggart, or possibly, as a liar.

We do not recommend that you oversell yourself, but we do recommend that you prepare so that you can answer confidently, factually, and accurately. A convincing and persuasive answer should include examples and illustrations, as in the following example:

Question by Interviewer: "Your statement of objective in this résumé indicates your desire to get into sales work. What experiences and knowledge do you have in selling?"

Answer by Applicant: "My first experiences in sales work began when I was 15 years old when I was asked by a friend to take over his newspaper route. Keeping his old customers, I was able to add new customers to my route until it doubled in size.

Another type of part-time sales experience occurred when I was 18 years old and went to work for Mr. Maustin at Maustin's Men's Clothing Store. Selling men's suits, especially during our sidewalk sales, taught me some things about. . . ."

Hypothetical as this example is, it stands in marked contrast to the empty answers that preceded it. The point is, you must explain to the interviewer what job skills you have to sell. You should do so by providing concise but memorable examples: illustrations, or stories about your factual background—experiences, knowledge and skills, interests, and abilities.

In summary, you can begin this second step by taking a single sheet of paper and making a factual list. List the facts with care, noting the exact dates, places, and names connected with your educational and work experiences. Then, as we have pointed out in Chapters One and Two, the best way to prepare for this personal briefing of yourself is to prepare your letter of application and professional résumé carefully. After completing summaries of your background and education, you must be prepared to offer something more. Be prepared to explain through examples and illustrations topics such as the following:

1. My most valuable educational experiences.
2. My most rewarding work experiences.
3. My most successful projects, accomplishments.
4. My strengths and capabilities.

Step 3: Research: Investigate the Company

The third step is to investigate the company and to find out all you can about it. This step has long range consequences to your career and to your investment in the company. If you do go to work for them, you may spend many years of your career with the firm. Things which seem unimportant now (such as growth potential, opportunities for advancement, and changing working conditions) may become vitally important to your reputation and career several years in the future.

Frequently, interviewers ask "Why do you want to work for *our* company?" This may be a difficult question for an interviewee to answer. You may not be able to convince him that you do want to work for his company. What's more important is that you answer this question for yourself and first convince yourself that this is the company *you* want to join.

Several questions should be raised to indicate some of the things you might want to research in a company before becoming an employee.[2]

___

[2]See Table 2 at the end of Chapter Four for a New Job Profile—a checklist of considerations to apply to employers and companies.

TERMS AND CONDITIONS:

1. How does this company treat its employees?
2. Is there opportunity for advancement here?
3. What are the expectations leading to promotions?
4. Are the working conditions safe, desirable, comfortable?
5. Does the company provide adequate salary and fringe benefits (i.e., insurance, retirement plans)?
6. Is the overall salary schedule competitive? (Are there hidden compensations? Stock options? Discounts? Housing available?)
7. Are the hours (overtime) acceptable? Are there lunch facilities? Paid holidays?
8. Are there provisions for sick leave, personal leave, maternity leave, vacation time?
9. Does the company expect employees to be mobile, to travel, and to relocate?
10. Are there extra-duty expectations for employees or off-duty standards?
11. Does the company expect me to provide my own car? Equipment? Tools? Uniforms? Or materials? Do they prohibit me from using my own? Are they insured? Compensated for?
12. Does the company provide me with parking facilities, office space, work areas?

COMPANY STANDING:

1. What is the company's history? (E.g., why, where, and when was it founded?)
2. What are the company's main products? Subsidiary lines? Services?
3. What types of equipment, facilities, and jobs does it have?
4. Is it part of a parent organization or does it have branches of its own? Where? What types? Plants? Offices? Stores?
5. Who are the company's biggest competitors? What do they have to offer or what advantages do they hold over this company?
6. What is this company's reputation? How does the company compare with its competitors?

7. How many employees, with what types of training, does the company employ? Type of employees?

8. What are the company's future plans and prospects for growth? What are its goals? Problems?

9. What are the company's expectations, traditions, and regulations? Liberal? Conservative?

10. What is the company's financial profile? Financially sound and stable? Size of payroll? Money problems?

11. Who owns the company? Major shareholders? Location of majority of stocks?

12. What is this company's growth potential? It is likely to grow with you? Merge with others? Go defunct? Split?

LOCALITY AND ENVIRONMENT:

1. Does the locality fulfill my needs and those of my family?

2. Does the community provide the things I value in terms of churches, schools, recreational facilities?

3. What is the cost or level of living compared to that to which I am accustomed?

4. Could I find desirable housing?

5. Is the climate satisfactory, desirable, tolerable?

6. Would my family integrate easily into the social and cultural realms in the community?

7. Would my family be accepted here?

8. Are there educational opportunities here for my own training or educational advancement?

The analysis provided here of the company—its terms and conditions, standing, locality, and environment—is only a beginning to a thorough investigation. You may be thinking that it would be impossible to investigate the answers to all these questions prior to taking an interview. You may be right. Time limitations and the lack of available information may make such explorations unfeasible, if not completely impossible.

However, there is a great deal of information about a company and its locality one can gather in a short period of time if one knows how to conduct such research.

Conversing with friends who work there, or chatting with other employees, can give you much insight. You may uncover management-labor problems or an impending strike. You may discover the regard (or lack of it) the employees have for the firm, or the acceptance (or lack of it) the company enjoys in the community.

Another valuable source of information to help you in your research of the company is the corporation's annual report. The report is likely to include the accountant's report, financial statements for the year, letters to the stockholders from the president or chairman of the board, a directory of the divisions, and a complete list of the names and business addresses of the officers and directors. Some of the more colorful annual reports may include photo features of the company's products and a pictorial review of the operations.

If you are fortunate enough to be able to visit the company, you will be able to get much first-hand information about its locality and environment.

A weekend or vacation trip to the plant site can tell you much about the community and its social, cultural, and recreational offerings. You don't have to take a banker to lunch to learn about the community, but you may want to chat with business-men. If you plan ahead, you may get a visitor's pass and a tour of the company.

But suppose that you do not have access to a firm's annual report, and that you do not have the opportunity to visit. What can you do then? The answer to this question might be found in your hometown library. Most libraries have such reference books as the *Thomas Register of American Manufacturers* and the *Thomas Register Catalog* file which classify and rate thousands of companies in the United States. Another description of American firms can be found in the *MacMillan Job Guide to American Corporations*. A publication entitled *25,000 Leading U.S. Corporations* provides rankings among U.S. manufacturers; and here you will find information regarding company name, city, state, sales, net profits, total assets, depreciation per common share, earnings, cash flow, and so forth. If you need the names and addresses of company heads, try *Standard*

and Poor's Register of Corporations, Directors, and Executives.
Moody's Industrial Manual will tell you about the company's
stockholders, about employees' consolidated sales and earnings,
and about its stock options.[3]

If, however, you do not have access to the reference section
of a library, there is much investigating you can do in the living
room of your own home. A copy of the *Wall Street Journal*
or *Business Week* may provide some interesting reading about a
company, its stock, its products, or its financial trends. You
might find your company described in *Fortune* magazine's
"500" review. A letter to the company's personnel office may
bring to your door recruitment brochures and advertising
materials used by the company. If you want to investigate the
community outside the company, write to the Chamber of
Commerce. They will send you information about churches,
cultural activities, scenic attractions, and recreational facilities.

Where and how can you find out about the level of living,
the cost of rentals, real estate, food prices, or the type of shopping available in the community? Try several copies of the
community's newspaper. If you have several daily editions or a
Sunday edition of the community's newspaper sent to your
home, you will have a quick guide to the cost of living differences between your community and the one to which you may
be moving. Have the person who does your grocery shopping
check the food prices, the weekly specials, the restaurant ads.
Look at the availability of apartment rentals or homes for
sale. If the newspaper does not include a multiple-listing section
for real estate, write to a local realtor, bank, or savings and loan
company for housing and financing information.

All in all, there is much research that you can do in investigating potential employers. You can discover the company's terms
and conditions, its standing, its locality and environment. You
can learn much about its products, its branches, its subdivisions,
its financial status, the type of work and careers it offers, and
the type of working conditions that prevail there. You can learn

[3]A list of reference books which describe U.S. businesses and corporations,
their directors and executives, is found in Appendix B.

these things through interviews or conversations with individuals who have knowledge of the company. You can learn these things by visiting the company and community. You can learn from the company's literature and reports. You can research in your local library or have reading materials sent to your home.

Step 4: Company Briefing: Prepare to Discuss the Business

The results of Step three should provide you with an abundance of information. In sorting through these materials you will feel the need for organizing them. You may want to classify them into a pattern which could form the answer to an interviewer's question. Suppose you were asked, "What do you know about our company?" At this point, you will want to speak knowledgeably. If you have briefed yourself well, you will know the names of the key people in the organization. You will know much about the company and its products. Of course, you do not want to sound like a know-it-all, but you do want to demonstrate that you were interested enough and cared enough to do your homework regarding the company.

Your answer about the company might follow an organizational pattern such as the following:

Answer: "Well, I read in your recruitment folder that Ames is an old established firm, founded in the late 1880s, but that it wasn't until the early 1950s that you added the business machines branch. And there was a letter from your president, Mr. Sanderson, in the annual report which pointed out that the company is planning building a plant in Toronto that, for the first time, would add an international dimension to the firm. I don't know if that means the company will want some of its American employees to live in Canada or not. . . ."

An answer such as the one above may not reveal many things about you, but it does demonstrate that you are interested enough to invest a little time and study in this company. The interviewer can't help but be impressed that you have done your homework. Such an answer could also be a clue to the interviewer that you are the type of person who studies a situation before getting involved—that you are a person who wants to learn, a person who is thorough. Also, you have shown the interviewer that you are not there to waste time. You do not have to be spoon-fed information that is available elsewhere. Thus the interviewer can conduct the interview on a higher level, and perhaps provide you with more advanced information than is given to less prepared applicants. The interviewers are also aided, in that they can now pattern their remarks by responding to the questions you raise.

If you know that you are going to participate in an employment interview, it makes good sense to brief yourself in advance about the company's history, products, types of operations, and work. It will make you more knowledgeable, confident, and impressive.

Step 5: Evaluation: Study the Situation

Studying the job advertisement and the job description, if there is one available, is most important to thorough interview preparation. You will want to have the confidence that the job you are applying for is a good one. If you have doubts about the job or the company, it may be wise to check with someone who has worked for the firm or someone who actually holds, or has held, the position for which you are applying.

One Friday afternoon a young man came bursting into my office absolutely filled with excitement and enthusiasm. He had responded to an advertisement which offered an "impressive executive opportunity" and he was going to be interviewed for it. By Monday morning his optimism was gone. The job was not all that he had thought it would be.

"If I had known then what I know now, I would never have applied for it," he said in disgust.

If there are want ads that mislead and deceive, if bogus positions are advertised, or if candidates are promised fantastic incomes, when in fact they cannot earn enough to meet expenses, then there is bound to be frustration and disappointment among job applicants. Beware the position that promises huge earnings in the form of commissions, but requires you to invest your money, automobile, or expenses. It may be wise to check your doubts and suspicions about the job or about the company with the local Better Business Bureau.

As you read the job description, and then study it carefully, questions about the nature of the work or the responsibilities involved will come to mind. You will want to jot these questions down so that you can ask them succinctly during the interview. You will want to do likewise with questions pertaining to the terms and conditions of employment. The job description is an aid to the candidate with the trying task of getting information and raising questions.

Another reason for studying the job description is to evaluate the qualifications and requirements of the job. Although it may be too soon to make a final decision, it is time to begin to evaluate you—with your personality, skills, experience, knowledge, educational background, and qualifications—against this position—with its characteristics, nature, responsibilities, and requirements.

There are three questions you should begin to answer. They may be asked you by others; but more importantly, you should be able to answer them for yourself. The questions are:

1. You want to work for *that* company?
2. You *want* to work for that company?
3. *You* want to work for that company?

The first question implies something wrong with the company in comparison with other companies. These company acceptability considerations should have been made at Steps 3 and 4 of the process. If the company has a bad reputation for whatever reason—inferior products, unreliable guarantee, poor service, shoddy workmanship, exorbitant prices, unfair treatment to its employees—you should know about it.

The second question implies something wrong with the job. If the particular job has a bad reputation (so that you should not *want* it unless you were forced to take it), you ought to know the factual nature of that reputation. Are there intolerable working conditions, or greatly undesirable side effects of the work, such as social criticism, health hazards, safety risks? Would taking the job put you in an untenable position in any way? Are the job and salary worth it?

We do not suggest that you always look for the "absolutely safe" job or for the one with little or no challenge. We do suggest that you begin to evaluate the job by analyzing the job description and raising additional questions about its nature and suitability to you.

The last question, number three, raises the point of your suitability to the position. Are you well suited to this job? Once again, the job description will give you some clues. Are the requirements of this job well suited to the personal qualifications which you have? You should not want a job for which you are not at all qualified.

An article in *Management Review* points out that twenty percent of the management work force in the United States is usually in a state of flux. As these hundreds of executives move from one job to another,, the article points out, landing the wrong executive job is relatively easy. Hundreds do it every day. Landing the right job is the challenge.[4] The job description should help you decide.

If, in your evaluation of the job description and in answering the preceding questions, you have doubts and questions, jot them down and find an appropriate time in the interview to raise them. It will give the interview greater purpose and meaning for you.

If, on the other hand, you can say that you do desire this position because you do respect the company and because you

---

[4]See John R. Clarke, "Landing That Right Executive Job," *Management Review*, 64 (August 1975), 31-36.

feel that the job is right for you, and you for it, you will approach the interview with much confidence.

"Know what you are applying for!" This bit of advice, a reoccurring theme in this book, is critical to good interview preparation.

Step 6: Anticipate: Get Set Through Rehearsal

Building confidence through rehearsal is the final step in interview preparation. The rehearsal is your opportunity to put the final touches on your preparation. It is also a time to pre-view or anticipate what may occur during the interview. Be-cause it is a preview, it is important for you to develop an attitude of confidence—to see yourself as a successful partici-pant. This does not mean that you should see yourself as "being amazingly impressive to interviewers who give you fantastic acceptance and great job offers with each interview." Such a view is pure fantasy, unrealistic reverie, or daydreaming. Positive rehearsal means that you see yourself as one who can answer questions with reasonable thoroughness, as one who can admit not knowing the answer to a question without getting flustered or losing poise. It does mean seeing yourself as a positive and active participant answering and asking questions to the best of your ability.

You may be thinking that a thorough rehearsal is impossible for an interview. In this sense, andd to that degree, you are correct. Because you do not know what will be asked of you, and because you do not know which facts or ideas will be presented about the company or the job, a rehearsal should not be expected to replicate the actual interview.

However, if you anticipate some of the actual needs and characteristics, you can plan to influence the interview to a greater extent. For instance, you should:

1. Consider your appearance and dress accordingly. Your appearance will likely make the first impression on the inter-viewer. You will want to groom yourself and dress so that you

feel confident with what you are wearing (a favorite suit or dress) while appearing in appropriate apparel to the interviewer. If you are concerned about whether your grooming is too liberal or too conservative, settle in favor of the conservative side. The last thing you want is to feel self-conscious or worried about your clothes at a time like this. "Appropriate" dress and grooming is the general rule because what is "appropriate" is often dependent upon the situation, the type of work, and the style of grooming and dress customarily worn in that type of work. You want neither to over dress nor to dress too casually or informally. Your grooming, dress, and personal cleanliness should suggest to the interviewer that you are neat, and that you are concerned about your appearance and its effect upon others without being faddish or distractive.

2. Anticipate the need for back-up information; and be prepared to bring extra copies of your résumé with you, in case the interviewers have forgotten their copies.

3. Anticipate the need to jot down notes from time to time and bring with you both pen and paper.

4. Anticipate your tendency to be overly serious and tense and plan to remember to smile and be poised.

5. Anticipate the types of questions that you will be asked, and think through the "sense" of your answers as well as possible examples and illustrations of them. For example, you can anticipate questions about your experience, training, and education, and questions about what you already know about the company and the job. You can rely on your self-briefings in Steps 1 and 4 of your preparation. Practice answering questions that are bound to arise.

6. Anticipate your role as a questioner in the interview. Practice asking the questions that you have prepared regarding the company, the job, and the community. Put them in a tone of genuine interest—a tone which suggests a real desire to learn more.

Rehearsals may be conducted orally in front of a mirror or practiced with a friend. This technique used by public speakers is a type of rehearsal which gives you some accurate feedback—

some information about how you sound and look to the interviewer. Another type of rehearsal is the silent, thoughtful *intra*-personal dialogue that goes through your mind as you preview in your mind what you anticipate will actually happen. This type of rehearsal can be conducted while you walk down the street or ride in the car.

WHAT CAN BE SAID IN SUMMARY ABOUT PREPARATION?

If you understand the purposes and types of employment interview you are engaging in, and if you follow the six steps of preparation, you will direct your energies toward more constructive means of developing confidencce in the employment interview. You will be more confident because you will be more competent to participate and more committed to fulfilling your informational and persuasive objectives. You will be a more interested and active participant in the employment interview, and thus you are more likely to get the position which is right for you.

CHAPTER FOUR

Participating in the Employment Interview

You should look forward to the opportunities provided by the employment interview. If you have followed the suggestions in the preceding chapters, you have prepared well. This interview is what you have been working and hoping for. It is an exciting challenge. You are fortunate to get such an invitation.

WHAT'S THE RIGHT APPROACH?

We are suggesting that you approach the selection interview with as much self-confidence as you can muster. No matter how many times you may have failed to secure a position in the past, you must now approach this interview with the attitude that you have just as good (if not better) a chance to succeed in getting the job as any other candidate. After all, each applicant is unique in terms of his personality and the personal qualities which that person can bring to the job. Your combination of personal characteristics, knowledge, and skills may be just what is being sought for this position.

So now an employer, the employer's representative, or a potential coworker is about to meet with you for a preplanned conversation with a structure and a purpose (the interview). Because you are the guest and the interviewer the host, you may feel that it is the interviewer who is responsible for structuring the interview—for beginning, conducting, and ending it. To a large extent, you are correct in this assumption. You may also feel that the interviewer is the important one in that he or she doesn't really need to fill the position; but you can't get the position without the interviewer's help. "I am really on-the-spot," you may self-consciously reflect to yourself.

But let's reverse that attitude and take a different posture or perspective. It is not you who is on the spot. It's the interviewer. The interviewer has a problem. The interviewer or the interviewer's sponsor has gone through a long, time-consuming, and expensive process to bring this interview about. The process involved planning, advertising, steps in assuring affirmative action procedures, writing a job description, consulting, and a host of other chores. Now, after weeks of such administrative planning, the interviewer must make it all worthwhile by selecting the best person for the job, by making a determination. The interviewer must make a recommendation (to hire or not to hire—that is the question) and be able to back up that recommendation with evidence and reasoning. In order to justify the cost in time and expense and to reach the organizational objectives, the interviewer wants to meet excellent candidates and to choose the best person for the job.

You can help that interviewer to choose *you* through your information and persuasion. This is your chance to provide the interviewer with the evidence and good reasons (that is, with the case) for hiring you. If you succeed in doing so, you will be an important and active participant in the interview. You will influence the course of the interview; you will be central to its success.

HOW DO YOU APPEAR, VERBALLY AND NONVERBALLY?

Your presence at the interview is likely to be the first physical meeting that you have had with the interviewer. Your letter of application and résumé have provided a word picture of you.

From these written materials your future employer most likely formed a mental image of you. Do you think your physical presence presents an image consistent with the employer's mental picture of you? Chances are that if you were invited to participate in the interview, your letter of application and résumé were successful. Something in that written communication must have interested someone in you. Now, you must capitalize on that advantage by having your spoken communication reinforce and supplement that favorable impression.

If we can assume that your interviewer is a good listener, then your verbal comments and responsiveness throughout the interview will provide much of the data regarding your experience, training, skills, and qualifications. However, as we have said, the primary purpose for the interview is to find out what kind of a person you are. Much of this information is provided nonverbally.

If you are truly a happy or pleasant person, you are more likely to reveal it through your smiles or laughter than through talk about these qualities of personality. If you are outgoing, friendly, and talkative, these qualities will likely be revealed more by how you appear than by what you say. If you are a good listener, you may not mention the fact, but it will show. The point is that the bulk of what we communicate about our social selves is observed more through our nonverbal messages than through the meaning of our words.

It is important for us to accept the interviewer as an ally. Our smile, handshake, and greeting should be warm and cordial. It is not enough to *be* interested; we must *show* our interest and enthusiasm. (You will recall that lack of it was the chief complaint of interviewers.) It must show in our posture, and in our facial expressions, in our eye contact, gestures, and movements. It must show in the rate, tone, and quality of our voice. What must show?

There are at least three levels of congruency involved here. First, the verbal and nonverbal image of ourselves must match that which we described in writing. For example: If, in our letter of application, we described ourselves as having salesmanship ability with a capacity for easily meeting and accepting people, then there ought to be evidence of those qualities in our demeanor in the interview.

A second level of congruence should occur between what we say (verbally) and what we show, nonverbally. For example, if we say we appreciate the interviewer taking time to meet with us but simultaneously we appear to be ill-prepared for the interview and we waste time, then we are not being verbally and nonverbally consistent. Our words may say, "I'm interested, I'm concerned"; but these verbal signals may be contradicted nonverbally by expressions which say "I'm bored."

A third level of congruency exists between nonverbal cues. If our posture and facial expressions suggest that we are patient and understanding but our swinging foot and tapping fingers suggest that we are impatient and moody, we have contradicted ourselves nonverbally.

Ultimately, we hope that both verbally and nonverbally we fit the mental image the interviewer holds of the person best suited for the job. This matching image theory is an important one, as we shall see in the cross-examination sequence of the interview.

WHAT ARE THE DIFFERENT STAGES IN THE SELECTION INTERVIEW?

Employment interviews may be analyzed by dividing them into six stages. These stages include:

1. the reception–acceptance phase
2. the EE response period
3. the ER briefing stage
4. the cross-examination sequence
5. the negotiating interval
6. the summary and leave-taking points.

Obviously, not all interviews have all six stages. The screening interview, for example, may have as few as three (Stages One, Two, and Six). Those which do have all six may have a highly disproportionate amount of emphasis on one or two stages and only touch upon the other phases. However, if you engage in several interviews with several different interviewers—whether for one job or several—you are likely to encounter all six stages at one time or another. The following descriptions should help you to identify these sometimes distinct stages. They are offered here neither in a necessarily chronological order nor in order of increasing or decreasing importance. Our analysis of the stages of the employment interview is offered here to provide an understanding of and perspective on many of the things that do happen in typical employment interview situations. The goal is greater information for the purpose of using it better. At each phase, suggestions will be made for improving your participation in the interview.

Stage 1: The Reception-Acceptance Phase

"Who are you? Oh, you're the applicant for the job opening." Being recognized as a serious applicant for a position is not as easy as simply calling yourself a serious job applicant. For one thing, you have to be recognized and accepted as an applicant by others who have many other concerns and interests on their minds.

To illustrate the point, we frequently have students in our interviewing classes keep track of the number of interruptions which occur during the course of an interview. One student (who had prepared well by making an appointment well in advance and confirming it by telephone) counted 14 interruptions during a 20 minute interview. These interruptions included telephone calls, office intercom buzzers, and people walking in and out of the office.

Do not assume that interviewers are always as prepared, ready, and willing to see you as they should be. The following are a few suggested details to get you off to a good start in this important initial phase.

Come *alone,* not *along.* It may seem comforting to you to have a member of your family or a friend along; but unless others are invited and arranged for, the presence of an "extra" can create an uncomfortable or awkward situation. The interviewer now has to think about what to do with your friend rather than thinking about what to do with you. Asking another (non-employee or non-applicant) to "sit-in" on the interview is taboo. Remember, this is a *private* conversation with a purpose involving the private business of the company and you. Do not leave the impression that you lack independence or that you are so insecure that you need someone along to provide moral support.

Come appropriately dressed and groomed for the occasion. Do not smoke or chew gum unless invited to by the employer, and then only if the interviewer will join you in so doing. Some interviewers regard this conversation as a formal meeting. It is not up to you to detract from that tone unless you have good reason to do so. Your personal habits will be observed. Your appearance (image) should suggest that you are ready to work.

Come early, or on time, but never late. If you are late for your first appointment, you may give the impression that you would be so habitually. The advantages of planning to arrive early include compensating for delays, overcoming the unexpected, and giving yourself time to get set. The desirable practice of arriving a day early and learning about the location and environment was discussed briefly in the previous chapter.

Bring a copy of any correspondence inviting you to the interview. Bring an extra copy of your résumé as well as pen and paper.

Upon your arrival, state your name and the purpose of your business. You cannot assume that others have been briefed on the purpose of your meeting or accurately informed of the time. On the other hand, you may be required to complete application forms, questionnaires, and so forth.

Greet your interviewers by name, whenever possible, and take your cues from them. Respond to introductions with a pleasant smile and a firm handshake (if a hand is extended). Wait for an invitation—by word or gesture—to sit down. Your interviewer may take you to another room to conduct the interview, or to meet other employees.

Seemingly minor details such as these may have a major impact during this introductory stage of the interview. One psychiatrist, Leonard Zunin, has suggested that it is the first four minutes of most of our personal meetings that provide the greatest number and most lasting impressions of ourselves to others.[1] If Zunin's perspective is correct, acceptance or rejection may occur early in the interview.

Social amenities, personal regards, the ice-breaking comments usually characterize this phase of the interview. Because your personal characteristics are often linked with your attitudes and your name, be certain that you express warm, positive feelings.

For example, it would be appropriate to respond to the introduction with a statement such as the following: "Thank you for meeting with me. I've been looking forward to this interview. It's nice to be here."

Be certain that your interviewers know your name (correctly pronounced last name), your purpose, and exactly which position you are applying for. Ask if they have received your résumé and immediately offer to provide another or to supply any additional information.

Most interviewers will spend this first phase of the interview in establishing rapport with you. Sometimes they will ask you some general ice-breaker questions in order to determine your mood, attitude, and general disposition. You might expect some general questions for openers such as, "How was your trip over here today?" A one-word response from you, such as "Fine," is not what the interviewer is trying to accomplish. On the other hand, a long-winded or negative blow-by-blow account of how—"the car wouldn't start . . . I got lost . . . traffic was terrible . . . parking impossible . . . the office was hard to

[1]Leonard Zunin, M.D., *Contact: The First Four Minutes* (New York: Ballantine Books, 1974), p. 6.

find"—is not what you want to present either. By a *positive* response, we do not mean to encourage those insincere, saccharine comments about how "perfectly wonderful the weather is . . . and how perfectly marvellous the highways are and how beautifully gorgeous the building in which we are meeting is."

Responses should be positive, but sincere, and neither too brief (suggesting abruptness) nor too loquacious (suggesting excessiveness). If it appears that the interviewer is simply attempting to make some "small talk," a terse and lucid story (e.g. "A funny thing happened to me on the way to the subway") may be in order and reveal both your sense of humor and your fluency.

Still other interviewers spend little time (especially in screening interviews) on introductions, breaking the ice, or building rapport. They are likely to move quickly into the second stage of the interview.

Stage 2: The EE Response Period

The EE response period is the "getting-down-to-business" stage in which the interviewer begins to ask more specific employment-like questions of the interviewee (EE). Many times these questions are taken from the application blank. They may also be thoughts gleaned by the interviewer while reading your résumé or letter of application.

Two types of questions you will want to distinguish between are the open- and close-ended question. The close-ended question calls for a one or two word answer. You are not expected to say more unless there is an important qualification or extenuating circumstance needing explanation.

In this phase of the interview, you might expect close-ended questions such as the following:

A. Do you have a driver's license?
B. Do you own your own car?
C. Have you ever driven for long periods of time (four to eight hours) at night?

D. Where did you go to high school?

E. Did you ever take a typing course?

F. Which business machines have you operated?

Questions such as these do not require long detailed answers. A simple "yes" or "no" answer is often all that is wanted as the interviewer runs down the list of "facts about the candidate."

However, it is during this phase of the interview that candidates will often be asked *open-ended questions regarding qualifications:*

1. What training have you had that might help you in a job like this?

2. What qualifications do you have that make you feel you will be successful in this job?

Such questions cannot be answered with a single word or phrase. Curt answers should not be given. The interviewer needs help in determining your qualifications for this job. Provide specific names, dates, and places; but above all, present answers which are convincing. You will need to explain the nature of your training in terms of the skills needed in this job.

This same type of detailed specificity is needed in *answering open-ended questions regarding your experience.* You might be asked:

1. What kinds of experience or related jobs have you had in connection with this type of work?

2. How did your previous employers treat you?

This last question is particularly difficult. No employer wants to hear derogatory comments (scapegoating or bad-mouthing) about another employer. The logic of the reason is simple—if you have nothing but bad things to say about your last employer, you will *most probably* have nothing but bad things to say about your next employer.

Open-ended questions regarding your personality are often difficult for the inexperienced job seeker. The timid or insecure person is likely to feel embarrassed to answer questions such as the following:

1. What do you consider to be your best accomplishment?
2. What causes you to lose your temper?
3. What is probably your biggest failing?
4. How do you feel when you receive complaints about your work?

Self-disclosure (publicly revealing your personal thoughts and feelings about yourself) is most difficult for many people. Yet it is this type of insight, analysis, and openness that is needed to provide an answer which has good content. Interviewers frequently seek to discover what you are like as a person by asking you questions which reveal your concept of self.

For example, a young man recently came to us asking advice about a second chance interview. Bob said he was being graduated and really looked forward to a position with an international airline. "I really blew my interview with the airline last year," he said. We asked what made him think so and he said, "I was too honest; I told them the truth." "But you should be honest and tell the truth in an interview," we replied, "What happened?"

"Well," he went on, "the interview was going along fine. Then this lady interviewer asked me this stupid question. She was asking me about what kind of person I was and then she asked—'How would your friends describe you?' Well, I was too honest. I told her to go ask my friends if she wanted to know that. How was I supposed to know what my friends would say?"

In our analysis, this young man was confusing honesty and truth with refusal or inability to provide a thoughtful answer. We suspect that the interviewer was asking him about how he sees himself (concept of self), how others see him, and the difference between the two views. Failing to understand what was being asked him, this young man probably gave the impression that he was neither very perceptive nor introspective.

Open-ended questions regarding your professionalism also require thoughtful, convincing answers. Suppose you are asked the following:

1. Does your present employer know that you are interviewing for a different job?
2. Why did you leave your last job?
3. In what ways do you think this position will be any different from the last one you held?
4. How long do you plan to remain with us should you get this position?
5. What do you hope to be, professionally, five years from now?

A question such as one of these can be a snare and a pitfall if you have not thought through your answers carefully and consistently. You will also need to be able to express those thoughts with clarity. A one-word or one-phrase answer is not enough explanation to those questions because behind each one is an implied request to explain the reasons and rationale for your answers.

If you feel uncomfortable about this portion of the interview, review the Personal Inventory Checklist at the end of this chapter and re-do the personal briefing step.

Thorough preparation and review of your letter of application, résumé, and the suggestions in the previous chapter (your personal briefing) should help you meet this difficult stage of the interview. You might be wise to look over a list of frequently asked questions and quiz yourself in preparation for this phase of the interview.[2]

[2]In addition to the questions provided in this book, you may want to see "Questions Frequently Asked During the Employment Interview," as reported by 92 companies surveyed by Frank S. Endicott, Director of Placement, Northwestern University.

Stage 3: The ER Briefing

The ER briefing is that phase in the interview when the interviewer (ER) asks you what you want to know about the company. If you have done your research by both investigating the company and preparing to discuss it, you will be in a confident position. "What do you know about our business?" You can impress an employer by answering this question with the facts and knowledge you gained by doing your homework. Don't overdo it, though. You don't want to give interviewers the impression that you are a know-it-all or that you have nothing to learn. They will be impressed, too, by the type of questions you raise.

Frequently, employers will have arranged a tour of the business or plant. This tour, with an informative tour guide, can add much to your knowledge of the organization, and it may help you to raise good questions that you would not have thought to ask. During this tour you may stop to meet several employees, managers, or company officials. Do take an interest in what these people are doing, saying, and asking. They, too, may either be part of the interviewing team or among those asked for their impressions of you. For you, this is much more than the ordinary type of public relations tour conducted by many companies. If you are merely being entertained, you are probably not a serious candidate.

Following your tour or visit with other members of the company you may receive a briefing—if your tour guide hasn't already given you one—which outlines the structure of the organization, its various department functions, and the products or services in which it deals. If there is no opportunity for a tour, this stage of the interview may be recognized by the interviewer's statement, "Now, let me tell you a little about the company." Listen carefully to what is being said. You may have need to use such information soon in your decision-making.

If he is thorough, the interviewer will inform you on all the details and responsibilities of the job that were not spelled out in the job description. Withhold your evaluative comments. Let the interviewer brief you. Note where the interviewer's job description is consistent or variant with your view of the job or the job description.

Stage 4: The Cross-Examination Sequence

The cross-examination sequence, which often follows the tour or the ER's briefing, is begun when the interviewer asks, "Do you have any questions for me?"

This opportunity should not be wasted. Saying nothing does not demonstrate that you understand. It does not suggest that everything was made perfectly clear to you. This is the time to ask intelligent questions. Ask questions with both the informative and persuasive purposes of the interview in mind. This is the time to ask about things that were not clear or about which you need further information. It is also the time to let the interviewer know that you have done your homework.

If you feel uncomfortable with phases three and four, review the New Job Profile at the end of this chapter and rehearse the company briefing step.

For example, suppose you were to ask the following question: "What does the company policy clause on overtime mean when it states that 'periodic overtime opportunities exist'?"

Such a question suggests that (1) you are genuinely interested in the corporation; (2) you have taken time and care in reading about the company; (3) you are serious enough about the job to inquire about the terms and conditions of employment; (4) you are confident enough to see yourself as successful in the job; and (5) if hired, you would be one to volunteer eagerly for additional opportunities.

If those suggestions cannot be clearly derived from a single question, you should have a half dozen or so similar questions of your own regarding the goals of the company, the expectations for the position, the opportunities for expanding the position, and your own promotion and success with the company.

You might embarrass the interviewer by asking why the former holder of the position left the job. Don't overwhelm the interviewer. Don't put someone on the spot, but have enough ammunition to carry on a high level of dialogue.

With these questions you are likely to attract several cross questions as the interviewer asks: "Do you mean . . . Would you be interested in . . . Could you. . . .?" It is exactly this type of free exchange which brings clarity and understanding. You will feel both pleased and confident if this phase of the interview goes well.

If, in some rare instance, you truly have no unanswered questions at the beginning of this phase, you will then take a different tack. When the interviewer asks, "Do you have any questions for me?" you should respond with a summary statement. For example, you might say, "Well we covered my questions regarding *(x), (y),* and *(z),* and I found out about *and so forth.* Is there anything else *you* can think of that you want to ask me or that I should be asking you?"

Such a response demonstrates that you have been listening with good comprehension. It also signals that you are prepared to move on either to the negotiation stage or to the conclusion of the interview.

Stage 5: The Negotiating Interval

The negotiating interval, which is always omitted in the screening interview, but never in the final interview, is usually introduced by the interviewer. Often salaries are listed in the job advertisement or description. But, let us assume that there is no information available to you on those topics. It is the interviewer's responsibility to bring up the subject of salary, contract, benefits, commitments, duties, and responsibilities. It is advisable to take your cue from the interviewer unless you are absolutely sure that the interviewer has forgotten these matters, has assumed you already knew them, or is delaying unduly in bringing these topics up for discussion.

By bringing up the topic yourself, you risk missing that clear signal from the employer that you are the choice for the job and that management wants to come to terms with *you* at this time, rather than vice versa. You also risk giving the impression that you are concerned exclusively with money matters and that you are overly aggressive. The interviewer may not know the exact limits he can negotiate at the time of this interview. Don't push the interviewer into such an admission.

If you feel it is necessary to bring up the question of salary, you might do so by simply inquiring if there is a salary schedule for employees. Another way to introduce the topic of benefits is to inquire whether the employees are covered by a group insurance plan. If the interviewer doesn't pick up these cues, you may be wise not to press the matter.

Occasionally, the interviewer will be the aggressive one in terms of negotiating salary. "What kind of a salary do you expect?"

Could you answer a difficult question like that? This is no time for joking. You could plead ignorance and say that you are unsure. You could give a broad range estimate (e.g., "Somewhere between ten and fifteen thousand dollars annually"). You could say that you were hoping to earn about X amount of dollars per year. If you are changing jobs, you could quote your present salary and express your hope that you could increase your salary. You could use another device of retortmanship (answering a question with a question) by saying, "I am not certain about salary. What was the salary for this position originally?" You will probably feel more comfortable by having the interviewer cite a salary figure first and then discussing the matter from that figure. You may also feel more comfortable if you talk about "the salary of *the position*" or "the rate of pay for *the job*" rather than in the terms of "how much am *I* going to make." Another similar approach is to say honestly that you do not know how much the position pays and would rather not speculate. Then simply inquire, "Can you tell me at this time what the job pays or what the company is offering?"

All of this discussion is simply eliminated, however, if the salary is known from the outset. Your "homework" should include finding out what comparable salaries for the position are. You are then in a position to provide an estimate of what this position *should* pay.

In an unusual training exercise in our interview class, we asked three potential high school teachers to step outside in the hall. We gave each one an identical job description for a teaching position they would soon be qualified to fill at the local high school. One by one, we called them back into the room for a mock interview and asked them the same set of questions. No interviewee heard the others until that person was finished with the interview. The instructor, who played the role of high school principal-superintendent, asked each one to consider his current level of living, all expenses, and debts. The question in each case was: "What salary would you have to have from this teaching job in order to live comfortably?" The first student quoted a figure about two thousand dollars below the minimum salary level for that district. The second interviewee cited a figure which was somewhere in the middle of the entire scale (comparable to salaries of experienced teachers with permanent certification who had taught for about seven years). The last interviewee quoted a salary about three thousand dollars above the highest level on the salary schedule.

This illustration points out that an inexperienced job applicant's guess about a salary figure can be quite unrealistic. It also points out the need for job applicants to do their homework on such matters. The three student teachers should have looked at salary schedules for teachers in several locales and compared them.

Negotiable items are not restricted to the salary considerations above. There are a host of other items such as fringe benefits, insurance, retirement, expenses, working conditions, duties, and responsibilities that should be considered, explored, and discussed. Often some of these considerations are far more important than salary alone. Explore these items in your discussion and check them out. Many such items are highly negotiable.

"Are you prepared to accept an offer right now, if one is made?" This is another difficult question for job applicants. You may have a prior commitment or want to consult with your family. You may be unsure of the offer or its details. In either case, you should probably reply, "How soon would you need to know?" Few interviewers would deny you a little time to reflect or consult. However, in some cases there are time pressures on employers, also. What they may be asking you, without saying so, is: "Should we make you an offer and stop interviewing applicants or should we continue our search?" Of course, if you are absolutely certain and have been awaiting this offer, don't delay. Accept with pleasure.

By not responding as soon as you have decided, you risk losing the job to another. On the other hand, by accepting too quickly, you risk regretting your choice later. You may, by resigning shortly after you've accepted the wrong job, risk antagonizing your new (and *last*) employer. You may lose opportunities for positions better suited to you.

An approach you should consider is to get a deadline from the interviewer. If the deadline is impossible to meet, urge consideration for an extension. Explain, if necessary, the circumstances surrounding the needed delay. Reaffirm your interest, willingness, and desire. Ask them for a commitment. For example, "Would you call me when you reach your deadline?"

If the situation is reversed, the applicant might ask the interviewer, "When might I hear from you regarding *your* decision?" Sometimes, employers cannot release a contract or make a commitment prior to a given date. You should know about such deadlines or starting dates. You might also ask if you should call at a certain point in time in order to follow up on this meeting.

The negotiating interval may take much time, during one or several meetings, and involve several management personnel. You will be in a good position if you know what you want and have good reasons for wanting it.

Stage 6: Summary and Leave-Taking

Summary and leave-taking points are usually signaled by some sort of agreement. If the negotiations have reached the agreement point, a summary statement will often follow. The interviewer might say, for example, "Let's see what we have agreed upon. We will send you a letter of agreement . . . and you will plan to . . . is that right? Agreed?"

Such summary statements are the cue for leave-taking. You should take your cue from the interviewer. However, if the interviewer begins the leave-taking moves (e.g. a hand gesture of finality, shuffling papers, closing a folder, or standing up) before you are ready to depart, you might initiate the summary yourself. A final agenda item that is always in order is to agree on the time and place of the next meeting. You could say, for example, "Are we agreed then, that you will contact me by_____?" If the interviewer decides that they will call *you* (you should not call them), you should not fight that decision. To avoid the awkwardness that often accompanies leave-taking, plan a concluding statement (a wrap-up or closing) with a note of finality to it.

Your attitude will be correct if you thank the interviewer for meeting with you and providing you with the opportunity to be considered for the position. Customarily, a firm handshake and a "goodbye" marks the termination point. Unless absolutely necessary, do not continue conversation or return after that point. Leave behind with the interviewer a copy of your résumé or a current telephone number and the hours during which you can be contacted.

WHAT STRATEGIES ARE AVAILABLE?

No tricks are recommended. The procedure outlined here—consisting of thorough preparation, active participation, and honest evaluation—involves much hard work. Dedication and sincerity are two essential ingredients in this process. Your knowledge and your speech communication skills will help you immensely.

There are several approaches to that very important Stage one (the reception–acceptance phase). We recommend a business-like approach. Make an appointment if invited to do so. Confirm the appointment by telephone. Be prepared with an extra résumé in hand. Reintroduce yourself, if necessary, to make your name clear. Express appreciation for being allowed to meet with the interviewer. Explain your purpose clearly and precisely.

Stages two and three (EE response vs. ER briefing), if reversed, will often give the applicant an advantage. If the applicant is an active participant in the dialogue, the applicant can sometimes encourage the interviewer to provide more details about what qualities are being sought in this position. By manipulating these stages, the applicant can match (congruent theory) what is being sought by the employer with what the applicant has to offer.

The matching-image strategy in interviewing can be played another way, too. Suppose you find that what the interviewer wants is what you do *not* have to offer. If the interviewer is correct about those qualifications, you are applying for the wrong job and may as well thank him for his time and consideration and say "goodbye."

But suppose you think he may be wrong. Then, you might attempt to change his criteria. For example, you might say to the interviewer, "I suspect that you are looking for a much more experienced person for this position. My inexperience, however, may be an asset to you. I will learn this job the way *you* want it done and won't always be confused and telling you how it was done at some other place. Also, my lack of preconceived notions will help us work together. . . ."

The same type of counterarguments could be assembled for such barriers as:

1. "You may think that a local resident would be a better choice, but. . . ."

2. "Perhaps you think that a man could fill this position better than a woman; however, I am capable. . . ."
3. "You may be convinced that only the holder of a master's degree is qualified for this job. My qualifications, however, are such that. . . ."

Such a strategy should be used with care, however, and only when you are quite sure that you are considered a lesser choice or not qualified. It is a difficult strategy because it involves persuading the interviewer that his image of the job is incorrect and that this new view (your view) is more valid.

There are other interview strategies; but many are learned through experience, and all are perfected through practice in interviewing. Learning from your experience in taking interviews depends upon evaluation, the subject of the next chapter.

TABLE 1

Personal Inventory Checklist

A. Consider your personal and professional needs and goals. (What are my personal and professional needs and goals? Are they compatible?)

1. On what type of salary can I live comfortably?
2. What are my immediate financial needs?
3. Will my budget change in the next year or two due to debts, and so forth?
4. Could I work on a commission basis only or do I require regular equal salary payments?
5. Professionally, will I require immediate training? Is on-the-job training best?
6. Will I require more training or schooling in the next few years? Should I consider half-time work only while I complete my training?

7. Would I be wise to complete my educational program first?

8. Will taking a position now help or hinder me in reaching my career goals?

9. Am I too personally independent to ever be happy working for an employer?

10. Should I be thinking about going into business for myself at this stage in my professional career? Is that feasible?

B. Consider your interests and attitudes. (What am I really interested in doing professionally?)

1. Would I be happier working for myself or for others?

2. What are the types of things that have always interested me most?

3. Do I enjoy working alone more than with others? If with others, do I prefer being supervised or supervising others?

4. Do I prefer working inside or outside?

5. Do I enjoy traveling, or being on the road for long periods at a time?

6. Do I resent being away from home on weekends or for several weeks at a stretch?

7. Is my preferred work with machines or with people?

8. Which is more rewarding to me—manual or mental work? Combination?

9. Am I a planner or a doer? Do I enjoy paper work? Statistical or records keeping?

10. Do I enjoy debating with others or persuading them to accept my point of view?

C. Survey your past experience, education, and training. (Where do I possess the greatest amount of knowledge or skills?)

1. Have I ever had any success in selling? Did I enjoy it?

2. Is my background in any way unique due to family or experience?

3. In what did I succeed in school?

4. Where did I get my highest marks, most recognition, highest honors?
5. Do I have talent or skills in an extra-curricular or avocational area?
6. Do I have natural ability? A hobby that is saleable?
7. Have any of my past ventures been successful?
8. What have my past employers or job supervisors pointed out as my greatest assets?
9. If there were a job connected with my education and training, what would that job most likely be?
10. What has been my most rewarding experience? Should I be exploring job opportunities in that direction?

D. Consider your physical stamina and general health. (What are my biggest physical strengths and weaknesses?)

1. Am I capable of doing heavy lifting, climbing stairs, and so forth?
2. Do I get eye-strain or headaches easily from some types of activity?
3. Do I have allergies or hay fever that would prevent me from working in some climates or conditions?
4. Does air-conditioning (or lack of it) make working conditions intolerable for me?
5. Do I require quiet in order to concentrate and do my work?
6. Could I work in most outdoor temperatures? Weather conditions?
7. Do some types of office or plant lighting affect me adversely?
8. Would being on my feet or seated behind a desk for long periods of time bother me? Am I a "high-energy" type that needs to be active almost all the time?
9. Do I have special "handicapped" needs that must be compensated for?
10. Do I need frequent and regular breaks or can I work constantly for longer periods of time?

TABLE 2

New Job Profile

Consider the following items in evaluating future employers and employees in relationship to a given position with the company. Can you rate these items as being EXCELLENT/GOOD/FAIR/POOR/ or IMPORTANT* vs. NON-APPLICABLE (N/A)?

TERMS AND CONDITIONS

1. Does this company have clear job descriptions that make it clear what employees are expected to do?
2. What is the corporate climate of this company in relationship to and with inter-relationships with its executive staff, middle management members, and work force?
3. How does this company treat its employees?
4. What are the expectations leading to promotions?
5. Are the working conditions safe, desirable, comfortable?
6. Is the overall salary schedule competitive? (Are there hidden compensations? Stock options? Discounts? Expense Accounts? Housing available?) Is this a straight commission pay agreement or a regular payroll? Does company make deductions?
7. Are the hours (overtime) acceptable? Is there a lunch break? Are there lunch facilities? Compensations for overtime or additional expenses?
8. Are there provisions for sick leave, vacation time, and so forth?
9. Does the company expect employees to be mobile, to travel, and to relocate? Does the company pay travel or moving expenses?
10. Are there extra-duty expectations for employees or off-duty standards? Am I expected to reflect a certain company image in my style of living, dress, ethics, morals, or membership in social clubs?
11. Does the company expect me to provide my own car? Will I have a company car? Equipment? Tools? Uniforms or materials? Do they prohibit me from using my own? Are these things insured by the company? Compensated for?

12. Does the company provide me with parking facilities, office space, work areas?

13. Are there patent or copy rights which the company demands over my work or creations? Is there a strict privacy or secrecy agreement which I must sign?

14. Is there opportunity for advancement here? Does company provide variety in work? Am I forced to retrain periodically? Who pays for retraining?

15. Are the management-union relationships normal? Is there a long history of unrest, dissatisfaction, and strikes here? Is a strike imminent?

16. What is the quality of both management and labor (union) leadership?

17. What is the longevity of employees with company? Is there rapid turn-over? Or no turn-over?

18. Is the company undergoing vast changes in terms and conditions of employment? Why have previous employees left this job?

19. Is there a reduction in force (R.I.F.) or retrenchment imminent that might include the position for which I am applying?

20. What is the quality and ability of the supervisor or boss for whom I will be working?

COMPANY STANDING

1. What is this company's future? Is it growing, merging, closing?

2. What is the company's history? (E.g., Why, where, and when was it founded?) Ethics and Morals?

3. What impression does this company make? Do the buildings need repair? Are they deteriorating?

4. How many presidents has this company had recently? Is top management always in a state of flux?

5. What are the company's main products? Subsidiary lines? Services?

6. What types of equipment, facilities, and jobs does it have?

7. Is it part of a parent organization or does it have branches of its own? Where? What types? Plants? Offices? Stores? What is the relationship?

8. Who are the company's biggest competitors? What do they have to offer or what advantages do they hold over this company?

9. What is this company's reputation? How does the company compare with its competitors?

10. How many employees, with what types of training and capabilities, does the company employ? Type of employees?

11. What are the company's future plans and prospects for growth? What are its goals? Problems?

12. What are the company's expectations, traditions, and regulations? Liberal? Conservative?

13. What is the company's financial profile? Financially sound? Stable? Size of payroll? Money problems?

14. Who owns the company? Major shareholders? Location of majority of stocks? Ratings on bonds?

15. What is the company's growth potential? Is it likely to grow with you? Merge with others? Go defunct? Split? Discontinue certain lines, products, or operations?

16. Has this company had tax problems or does it have a pending law suit of major consequence against it?

17. Is this company likely to move, open, or close other branches, and so forth? Are there harmful rumors about expansion, merger, moving, and so forth?

18. How does this company handle corporate complaints?

19. Does the company stand behind the quality of its work with solid guarantees? Product pride?

20. Is this company overmanaged or undermanaged? Is the relationship between production and sales a good one?

ENVIRONMENT

1. Would the location of the company and the community provide a desirable place to live?

2. Does the locality fulfill my needs and those of my family?

3. Does the community provide the things I value in terms of churches, quality schools, recreational facilities?

4. Is the cost or level of living comparable to that which I am accustomed to?

5. Could I find desirable housing, or financing for housing, at a reasonable cost?

6. Is the climate (temperature) satisfactory, desirable, tolerable?

7. Would my family easily integrate into the social and cultural realms in the community?

8. Would my family be accepted here?

9. Are there educational opportunities here for my own training or educational advancement?

10. Will there be environmental changes here in the next few years to improve or impair the safety, beauty, desirability, or quality of life?

CHAPTER FIVE

Evaluating Employment Interviews

"How well did I do? Was this interview successful?"

These two questions often come to one immediately following an employment interview. One easy but erroneous answer is this: "It depends upon whether or not you got the job."

There are at least two reasons why such reasoning is erroneous: (1) Many employment interviews do not have, as their end, actually getting the job (i.e., sometimes they are screening interviews; perhaps they merely narrow down the number of candidates; or perhaps the company is not yet ready to make a final offer); and, (2) due to a variety of reasons you may have done an excellent job of participating in the interview but still not have gotten the job.

The counter assumption—"If you got the job, you must have done well in completing a successful interview"—is also erroneous. You may not have been quite "right" but were hired anyway (e.g., of all the candidates your minimal qualifications were best; or "someone upstairs gave you the nod"; or the decision to hire was not made on the basis of successful interview participation, and so forth).

A different perspective on this evaluation process may be gained by removing the evaluation of an interview from the "contest" or "game theory" perspective entirely. A good interview, after all, may have taught both you and the interviewer much. You both may have contributed, and had a great dialogue and interaction; but you both may have decided correctly that this job was not best suited for you. That's success, too! But if one can *not* judge the success of his or her interview on the basis of whether one was awarded the position, upon what criteria can an employment interview be judged?

Perhaps most of the remaining alternatives lie in that most important area of personal evaluation. Objective self-evaluation, as you shall see, can be made against a set of purpose-oriented criteria and a variety of common sense questions. If interviewing is thought of as a skill, or as a tool toward an end, rather than as a contest or an end in itself, we may be better able to evaluate it.

PROCEDURE

There are several steps one can take in making an evaluation of the employment interview:

1. *Reconstruct the interview* in your mind as soon after the interview as you can be alone and put some concentration into it.

2. *Make an outline* of the main topics discussed and write down on paper any impressions, no matter how subjective, that you can recollect.

3. *Make notes on the facts.* If you were able to jot down a few pertinent facts and figures during the interview, combine these notes with all the other facts you can recall. Your mental memo pad may not be accurate enough several hours or several days later.

Some job applicants who know they will be interviewing with several companies keep a file of facts on their interviews. The following is a brief sample. Key questions might be recorded on the reverse side.

The advantages of keeping such a file is that one can compare several opportunities, if more than one company makes an offer. It also permits you to review the facts and to keep a permanent record of the interview transactions.

```
                                    Date _____

     Company _____    Interviewer _____
     Address _____    Position _____
     _____    Telephone _____
     Telephone _____    Other Contact _____
          Position or Title of Position _____
     Duties: _____
     Job Description: _____
          Contract Terms $ _____ for _____
          Other Benefits _____ Pension: _____
     Insurance: _____
     Other Considerations: _____
     _____
          Opportunities: _____
     Notification Instructions and Date: _____
```

CRITERION QUESTIONS

After you have completed your outline and notes, recalled
from the actual interview, you are ready to begin applying that
information to the following questions.

A. Did I accomplish my purposes?
 1. If my purpose was to inform, did I provide all the necessary
    information to this interviewer and employer that I should
    have? If not, what other information should I have pro-
    vided?
    a. Did I answer all questions clearly and completely?
    b. Did I provide an extra résumé or other additional in-
       formation?
    c. Is there evidence that the interviewer listened to me well?
 2. Did I get the information that I needed about the com-
    pany position, duties, working conditions, responsibilities,
    salary, benefits, job security, and so forth?

a. Was this information reliable and accurate?

b. Can I check the validity, reliability, and accuracy of this information against other known sources?

c. Did I listen with good comprehension? Is there evidence of this? Do I now know what the company is looking for?

d. Were my questions clear and complete?

e. Were they the wrong or right questions?

3. Did I provide honest, accurate information about me—my abilities, background, training, experience, and so forth?

4. Was I asked for information that I couldn't provide or were there questions I couldn't answer?

5. Did I compensate for poor environmental factors in the interview situation? Did environment work against me or was I able to use it to my advantage?

6. Did I accept the interviewer's persuasive comments with an open mind?

7. Did I, later, consider the interviewer's persuasion critically? Did I find unwarranted bias? Inaccuracy? Inconsistency? Did I adjust my conceptions in lieu of this?

8. Did I have an adequate opportunity to persuade the interviewer?

9. Is there evidence to believe the interviewer understood and believed what I said?

10. Did I persuade, by impressing, by convincing, stimulating or actuating the interviewer? What evidence is there?

11. Was I successful in helping to structure the interview to my persuasive advantage?

12. Did this interviewer do a good job in working *with* me?

13. Was the interviewer successful informatively, providing data and asking good questions to provide me with an opportunity to inform?

14. Was the interviewer successful persuasively, convincing me and providing me with the opportunity to persuade?

15. Did I convince the interviewer that my training, skills, experience, and personality were congruent with job specifications?

16. Was the interviewer a help or a hindrance? Totally inept?

17. What were my areas of greatest strength in this interview?
18. What were my greatest failures or shortcomings in this interview?
19. Overall, would I rate this interview as good, fair, or poor?
20. What can I do to improve my next employment interview?

B. What impressions did I make?

1. Was I courteous to the interviewer, receptionist, and all concerned?
2. Did I handle well my arrival, introductions, and approach to the reception–acceptance stage?
3. Was I able to call interviewer or employer by the correct name? Correctly pronounced?
4. Was I patient in allowing the interviewer time to get set?
5. Did I help to put the interviewer in good mood?
6. Did I reinforce (verbally *and* nonverbally) the interviewer?
7. Did I make a good appearance in terms of posture, dress, and grooming for this position?
8. Was I appropriately on time and well prepared?
9. Did I speak forcefully enough but in a pleasant tone and with good visual contact?
10. Did I seem prepared:
    a. by asking good, informative and persuasive questions?
    b. by giving short answers for close-ended questions and thorough answers for open-ended questions?
    c. by illustrating a knowledge of myself, my goals, abilities, and so forth?
    d. by illustrating my (homework) knowledge of company and community?
11. Did I center my attention on the interviewer as well as on what I was saying?
12. Did I appear eager, interested, and enthusiastic?
13. Did I delineate my goals or was I too narrow?
14. Was my language appropriate? Did my word choice seem appropriate and correct?

15. Did I take an active posture and help to organize the structure and pattern of ideas to best advantage?
16. Did I show appreciation and gratefulness to the interviewer or other persons involved both at the beginning and end of the interview?
17. Did I show annoyance at interruptions?
18. Nonverbally, did I engage in autistic gestures (e.g. sprawling posture, fidgeting, playing with jewelry) that may have left a bad impression?
19. Did I make a good exit or was the summary-leave taking stage awkward?
20. Was my impression on the interviewer consistent with that stated in my written communication? Is it congruent with the image the interviewer holds for the job holder?

PROBLEMS IN THE EVALUATION PROCESS

The success of this entire employment evaluation process depends upon your objectivity. If you are too biased or too blinded by your own subjectivity to see your mistakes, this method will be of little or no value to you. You may need to have an objective third party evaluate your participation or your account of it. Of course, having an objective third party or a tape recorder present *during* the actual interview is most often impossible.

The answer to this problem may be to take a course in employment interviewing. Such a course is valuable in providing you with objective help in pointing out your mistakes and in helping you to improve upon them. Such a course will most likely contain mock interviews or practice sessions. The members of the class are likely to gather around a video tape recording of your interview and constructively point out your strengths and weaknesses. Such a session will often be followed by practice interviews during which you will be coached on how to make any necessary improvements. Weekend workshops in interviewing can also help one improve.

Another problem related to objectivity in employment interview evaluation is the illogical tendency to judge the company by the interviewers. Analysis of applicants' remarks following employment interviews reveals that job applicants tend to personalize the entire company by their impressions of the interviewers' personalities. It is not uncommon, for example, to hear a job applicant say, "Yes, I interviewed with the ZYX Corporation last year. They're not very interested in people outside their own corporate image. Actually the whole company is pretty cold and conceited."

Another type of comment often heard is, "I wouldn't want to work for that company. They treat their help like dirt."

Where are these impressions formed? How did the company get such a bad image? A little cross-questioning (interrogation) often reveals that this is one person's image of the entire company based upon a bad interviewing experience. Perhaps the job applicant's bad impression of the interviewer is reinforced by the story of another frustrated applicant or by a vengeful former employee who was fired.

In either event, it is unfair and illogical to judge the entire firm by a few bad impressions. This "allness" error in reasoning or "jumping to hasty generalizations" makes objectivity in interview evaluation impossible.

The counter bias is also a snare and a pitfall to objective evaluation. You may get the impression from an overly anxious, flattering job recruiter that you are absolutely great for the job and that the job is absolutely tailor-made for you. Again, don't let the interviewer's personality fool you about the company, the job, the situation, or your successful participation in the interview. What is the validity, accuracy, and reliability of the information and feedback I am getting from the interviewer? That is the question.

Even if it takes a little healthy skepticism to do it, hold on to your objectivity in making employment interview evaluations.

ADVANTAGES AND USE OF EVALUATIONS

No interview is complete without an evaluation of it. In addition to the summing up and evaluating that the interviewer must do, you, too, should be concerned about the success of the interview and the effectiveness of your role in it. Each interview you take can help you to be a more effective participant in the next interview.

There is a distinction that must be made here, however. Remember the story of the man who said he had had "ten years of experience on the job" and was contradicted with the explanation that he had only had "one year's experience ten times?" So it is with employment interviewing. We may say we have had experience with job interviews—having completed dozens of them. But unless we evaluated them in such a way that we learned from them, we may only have had experience with one interview dozens of times.

Learning from our mistakes, learning to improve our weak points and strengthen our assets, requires thoughtful, objective evaluation. Learning from our own mistakes can be a long, painful, and frustrating method of improvement. It may be faster, as well as less painful and frustrating, to learn from the mistakes of others. Reading a book on the subject is one way of improving. Discussing experiences with other job applicants and learning from their mistakes are other means. Ultimately, however, the learned changes (improvement) in your own behavior are your goal.

In addition to your improvement as an interview, you may also acquire, in the same way, greater understanding as an interviewer. You do not have to be a manager or a personnel officer to be called upon to help with the process of selecting new employees. As an employee on almost any job, you may be called upon from time to time to give your opinion on the suitability of a potential employee (job applicant) by engaging in an employment (or screening) interview. Evaluation of your own employment interviews, as an applicant, may give you a greater understanding and feeling for what the job applicant is going through when you are on the other side of the desk. The uses of good employment interview evaluation to personnel officers, managers, and supervisors are many and varied. They range from the initial steps of setting up screening interviews to welcoming new employees. But generally speaking, they, too, should learn greater skill and understanding on both sides of the employement desk.

THE ULTIMATE DECISION

So far this chapter has dealt with evaluating the employment interview. However, whether the interview was or was not successful and whether or not you were an effective participant are different questions from the ultimate one. That is, should I accept the position or not?

We assume that you will find a job which seems right for you. But how do you decide when the potential employer asks, "Well, do you want the job or not? Will you sign the contract or not?"

Assume that you have some time to decide. All the suggestions in the foregoing chapters were made to give you the best evidence available and to put you in the best position to make this decision. You may want to get additional advice or do some further checking. Eventually you may make your decision on the basis of the answers to two questions.

1. Is this position really well suited to me?
2. Does this position really offer what I want?

At that point, you will have made an important decision in your changing career.

CHAPTER SIX

Special Problems

"Special Problems" is the title we put on this chapter as a general label for some of the genuine concerns that job applicants have. Perhaps we should have entitled it 'Freqent Questions," because these concerns come to us in the form of inquiries that are most often very difficult to answer. We have patterned this chapter along lines similar to those along which the entire book is organized. The parts include problems regarding:

1. Letters of application and the résumé
2. Portfolios
3. Application forms
4. Employment interviews and questions of salary
5. References
6. One final opportunity—the thank you letter
7. A final word of advice

It is certain that we will *not* solve all these problems. We may fail to answer many of the questions. We can only hope to provide ideas which will help some of you to solve these problems and answer these questions for yourselves. We can only hope that an idea or two which we advance will help in the problem-solving process.

LETTERS OF APPLICATION AND THE RÉSUMÉ

Having read Chapters One and Two, you already have some insight into the preparation of letters of application and of the résumé. In helping others to prepare their materials we have encountered a variety of different concerns.

How Do I Know My Letter Includes Enough?   There is no one answer for this question. We do suggest that if you have prepared your letter carefully and have included just enough specific data to support your candidacy for the position then you have probably said enough. The ancient Greeks used to use a triad approach to build a point. Simply, it consists of stating a single point and then following the explanation of that point with three examples. This method may also be useful to you; however, don't use it monotonously. If you develop three areas of experience, then you may wish to use three specific examples to document each area of experience—more than three tends to be "over-kill." Remember, save some of your major points for the interview.

Most letters of application should be kept to *one* page. Thus an excellent test would be to ask yourself if you have written the finest statement you can in a one page limitation. Read to identify any unimportant items or statements—if any exist, eliminate them. Any irrelevant ones? If so, omit them. Have your spouse, or someone who knows you well, read your work to see if you have left something out. We do urge you to proofread your work carefully, even if it is prepared by an agency. You should be certain that nothing is included to your detriment, and that nothing highly significant is omitted. The final work is *yours*—regardless who prepared it.

"Killer Phrases."   Often applicants will include what we call potential killer phrases in their letters. Some employers—not all—get disturbed when they read phrases such as: "I hope to hear from you at your earliest convenience"; "I shall await hearing from you"; "I write in strictest confidence and trust you will respect my request"; "Mr. Harold Jones of your firm has suggested that I write to you" (when Mr. Jones should not have been serving as recruiter and you should not have used his name without asking first); or "My experience is unexcelled in the area of . . ." (well received when your employer is in the same area—but do avoid "allness" terms and superlatives about yourself). Whenever a phrase you have written doesn't sound quite right to you or to the person helping you proofread, be careful. Check it out. Be correct. Be positive. If in doubt, omit it.

Do I Have to Include My Marital Status Such as "I'm Divorced" or "I'm a Single Woman?"   There is no need to include marital status on most application blanks, although it probably won't hurt your chances for consideration in the majority of cases. There is no reason to include such information on your letter of application or résumé since you are in compl te control over what goes into it. Let the question be handled in the interview—if it should come up.

What Do I Write about My Health?   We have had several students with problems such as diabetes who have asked this question. There is probably no answer which would fit all situations. We firmly believe that most employers are becoming more knowledgeable and tolerant about such concerns. If an application form calls for such information, we would suggest that you include it with an added word, "controlled." If you are asked to discuss your health, do so openly and confidently. Nonverbally, you can suggest that any health problems which may exist do not "get you down."

"Gaps."   "But, sir, I don't want to include that three year period; and I don't want to talk about it." There are two kinds of "gaps" or omitted years in a résumé: accidental and intentional. Accidental omissions are the result of careless proofreading. If you should omit a period of time, it can be discussed in the interview. Intentional gaps are more challenging. In our experience we have found that such a person can use a summary of experiences or qualifications approach and leave the actual question about the gap for the interview. You should be prepared

to answer such a question when asked. More importantly, you cannot run away from your past no matter what the reason. If you are looking for a career, then remember that careers are built upon mutual trust between employer and employee. If your employer learns of a concealed period, you may find that it is impossible to retain his or her confidence. We know of few cases, if any, where honesty is not the best approach. The same is true of claiming credentials which you do not possess. We know of seven highly educated persons who were summarily dismissed for having falsified credentials. Such a reputation may follow you for many years; so it may be better to face up to the situation and sell yourself upon your potential—and then live up to your word.

We also urge you to heed the old expression, "never *leave* a job." That is, never become so dissatisfied that you literally slack off on your work, become a complainer, or walk off *(leave)* the job. The person who establishes himself as a griper and who manages only to find fault with his current position may well discover that he will find exactly the same faults in a future position. Be positive in your position and do your best no matter how troublesome the work conditions are. Then you can seek a new position without "burning your bridges behind you." You may need those recommendations to advance.

Priorities.   Priorities are a problem for numerous applicants. In the chapter on résumés, several suggestions were given. It is necessary for the experienced person and for the new graduate to review his attributes and then to set them forth so that his priorities become evident. As a rule, place your most significant experience first as well as your highest level of education. If you include your goals, then place them at the highest priority. Eliminate insignificant trivia and redundant materials.

Current Common "Goofs."   After all is complete, be certain to review again: Did I sign my name? Did I include my résumé with my letter? Did I address the envelope correctly? Did I place sufficient postage on it? Did I mail the letter or did I depend upon someone else to forget for me?

PORTFOLIO

A portfolio is a portable case for holding loose sheets of paper, art work, drawings, examples of cartography, photography, advertising design, stage design, news reporting copy, and other important types of documentation for possible review. From the above, it should be obvious that a portfolio is appropriate for a relatively small number of applicants. It is useful only to anyone who is in a career which requires a review of actual professional results.

A portfolio should be prepared with the utmost care. Select appropriate examples of your best work which reflect a range of your talents. For example, a costumer seeking a new position in theater might well select drawings which represent a variety of styles such as Shakespearean, ancient Greek, early American, or futuristic. In addition, a costumer might also include color photos of the final execution of the drawings to illustrate his ability to achieve the concepts designed. Such work should be carefully mounted on quality poster board and carefully labeled. Professionalism in the preparation of a high quality portfolio is a must. Unfortunately, it is not practical to include examples of such a file here.

Should your occupation lend itself to the use of a portfolio there are some considerations which become imperative. Assuming you have it fully prepared, we urge you *never* to mail an unsolicited portfolio. Based upon unfortunate experience with college teachers, we assure you that getting someone to return your important papers or work contained in a portfolio is often very difficult. As a rule, supply a portfolio only upon specific request, and even then, with caution. Be certain you really want to be considered for that position. It might take two or more weeks before such a collection will be returned. If you do mail such materials, remember that often they are original, or at least quite expensive to duplicate and to prepare, and must be sent by insured and registered mail. In addition, you *must* include specific instructions and sufficient postage for their return. We would even recommend that you request them returned by a specific date.

In the final analysis, you should realize that the use of a portfolio is essential for certain career fields. However, if at all possible, use it only at the actual face-to-face interview. The presence of the portfolio will provide additional opportunity for discussion of your work.

APPLICATION FORMS

Most business, governmental, educational, or other employers require the completion of one or more application forms. These forms may be brief and simple or quite complex—depending upon the employer's requirements. For your reference we have selected two application forms for study. The first (Figure 23), entitled, "Three Oaks Restaurant," illustrates what might be expected of an applicant seeking a beginning position. The second (Figure 24), which does not include the name of the firm for reasons of confidentiality, represents the type which might be required of a management level applicant or an applicant seeking a position with special requirements. Using these two applications as reference points, you may wish to consider such special problems as the following:

Immediate. Usually you will either receive an application in person at the employer's office or, upon request, through the mail. Remember, if you do go in person to seek employment, you should anticipate being requested to complete certain forms. You must be prepared in order to make a good impression and to avoid embarrassment.

Essentials. We suggest that you may want to consider taking a brief case with you containing the following: (a) a pencil and a good ball point pen; (b) a clip board or stiff folder; (c) a pocket dictionary; (d) necessary legal information such as your social security number, your driver's license, your certificate

APPLICATION FOR EMPLOYMENT

THREE OAKS RESTAURANT
77 U.S. Avenue
Albany Center, Illinois 60005

DATE_____ Social Security Number_____

Print name in full_____
First   Middle   Last

Address_____
Number   Street

City_____State_____Zip Code_____Phone_____

How long have you lived at this address_____

If you do not have a phone, is there someone who would give you a message?
Who?_____Phone Number_____

When were you born?_____
Month   Day   Year

Age_____Height_____Weight_____Sex_____
(M)   (F)

Check one: (Single) (Married) (Divorced)   Widowed)   (Separated)

Circle highest grade attended in school: 1 2 3 4 5 6 7 8 9 10 11 12

College?_____Business School?_____

Job Preference: (1)_____(2)_____

Are you interested in working: Full Time?_____Part Time?_____
Nights?_____Days?_____

Any defects in hearing?_____In vision?_____

Have you ever had a back injury, or are you subject to any kind of back trouble?_____
Are you subject to any kind of foot trouble?_____
Person to notify in case of accident:_____Relationship_____
Address:_____Phone Number_____

If married, what type of work does your husband or wife do?_____

List ages of dependents and relationship to you:_____
_____
_____
_____

Do you have any friends or relatives employed, or formerly employed, at the Three Oaks
Restaurant?___._____Names_____
_____

Have you served in the U.S. Armed Forces?_____

SIGNED:_____
Please sign your name as you would like it to appear on your pay check if hired.

PERSONAL HISTORY:

NAME: LAST   FIRST   MIDDLE   IF MARRIED, MAIDEN NAME

SOCIAL SECURITY NUMBER   HOME TELEPHONE NUMBER

LIST ALL HOME ADDRESSES IN LAST TEN YEARS. USE ADDITIONAL PAPER IF NECESSARY.   HOW LONG

PRESENT ADDRESS: NUMBER   STREET   BOROUGH   CITY   STATE   ZIP CODE   FROM

PREVIOUS ADDRESS: NUMBER   STREET   BOROUGH   CITY   STATE   ZIP CODE   FROM: TO:

PREVIOUS ADDRESS: NUMBER   STREET   BOROUGH   CITY   STATE   ZIP CODE   FROM: TO:

ARE YOU A U.S. CITIZEN?   YES ☐   NO ☐   IF NOT,

DATE OF BIRTH   WHAT IS YOUR CURRENT VISA STATUS _____

MARITAL STATUS: SINGLE ☐   ENGAGED ☐   MARRIED ☐   WIDOWED ☐   SEPARATED ☐   DIVORCED ☐

MALE ☐   FEMALE ☐   HEIGHT   WEIGHT

LIVE WITH PARENTS ☐   SPOUSE ☐   ALONE ☐   OTHERS?   RENT ☐   OWN HOME ☐

FATHER'S NAME: HOME ADDRESS   OCCUPATION

MOTHER'S NAME: HOME ADDRESS   OCCUPATION

SPOUSE'S NAME: OCCUPATION

SPOUSE'S DATE OF BIRTH: DATE OF MARRIAGE: NUMBER AND AGES OF CHILDREN

WHO REFERRED YOU TO THIS COMPANY?   HAVE YOU PREVIOUSLY MADE APPLICATION TO THIS COMPANY?

YES ☐   WHEN?   NO ☐

GIVE NAMES OF RELATIVES EMPLOYED HERE

IN CASE OF EMERGENCY NOTIFY: GIVE NAME OF PERSONS WHO CAN BE REACHED BY TELEPHONE DURING WORK HOURS.

NAME   ADDRESS   PHONE   RELATIONSHIP TO YOU

HAVE YOU EVER HAD YOUR WAGES ASSIGNED OR GARNISHED?   YES ☐   NO ☐

HAVE YOU EVER HAD ANY OTHER CREDIT JUDGEMENTS?   YES ☐   NO ☐

TYPE OF WORK DESIRED   MINIMUM SALARY REQUIRED $ PER

MILITARY SERVICE: WHAT IS YOUR PRESENT SELECTIVE SERVICE (DRAFT) CLASSIFICATION?

WHAT IS YOUR PRESENT RESERVE STATUS?

HAVE YOU EVER SERVED IN THE U.S. ARMED FORCES?   IF YES, WHAT BRANCH?

DATES OF SERVICE: FROM   TO   RANK AT DISCHARGE   TYPE OF DISCHARGE OR SEPARATION

HEALTH: HAVE YOU ANY PRESENT ILLNESS OR HANDICAP?   YES ☐   NO ☐
IF YES, PLEASE DESCRIBE.

HAVE YOU HAD ANY MAJOR ILLNESS WITHIN THE LAST FIVE YEARS?   YES ☐   NO ☐
IF YES, PLEASE DESCRIBE.

DO YOU MAINTAIN AN ACCOUNT WITH ANY BROKERAGE CONCERN?   YES ☐   NO ☐
IF YES, PLEASE GIVE NAME OF CONCERN.

Application
for
Employment

EDUCATION: LIST ALL SCHOOLS YOU HAVE ATTENDED.

SCHOOL	NAME AND ADDRESS OF SCHOOLS	DATES ATTENDED FROM	TO	DID YOU GRADUATE?	LIST DIPLOMA OR DEGREE
HIGH					
COLLEGE					
OTHER					

EMPLOYMENT HISTORY:

IN COMPLETING THE TABLE BELOW, PLEASE BEGIN WITH YOUR PRESENT OR MOST RECENT EMPLOYER. ACCOUNT FOR YOUR PAST TEN YEARS OF EMPLOYMENT. CHECK WHETHER PART OR FULL-TIME EMPLOYMENT.

NAME, ADDRESS AND TELEPHONE OF EMPLOYER	POSITION HELD AND NAME OF IMMEDIATE SUPERVISOR	FULL TIME	PART TIME	DATES OF EMPLOYMENT FROM	TO	TERMINAL SALARY BASE RATE	REASON FOR LEAVING
1.							
2.							
3.							
4.							
5.							
6.							
7.							

ALL FORMER EMPLOYERS WILL BE CONTACTED TO VERIFY THE ABOVE INFORMATION. MAY WE CONTACT YOUR PRESENT EMPLOYER? IF YOU HAVE EVER BEEN DISCHARGED OR FORCED TO RESIGN FROM A JOB, YOU MAY USE THIS SPACE TO EXPLAIN.

UNEMPLOYMENT:

ACCOUNT FOR ALL UNEMPLOYED TIME OF TWO OR MORE MONTHS AFTER LEAVING SCHOOL AND BETWEEN JOBS HELD.

DATE UNEMPLOYED FROM	TO	STATE WHAT YOU WERE DOING	GIVE NAME AND ADDRESS OF PERSONAL REFERENCE WHO CAN VERIFY THIS, NOT RELATIVES

PERSONAL REFERENCES: PLEASE GIVE TWO PERSONAL REFERENCES WHO ARE NOT RELATED TO YOU AND WHO ARE NOT FORMER EMPLOYERS.

NAME	HOME OR BUSINESS ADDRESS	OCCUPATION	YEARS KNOWN
1.			
2.			

Please answer each of the following questions. Use additional paper to explain "Yes" answers where necessary.

1. (a) Have you ever been bonded? .... Yes No

(b) Have you ever been refused a bond by a surety company? .... Yes No

(c) Has such a bond ever been denied or revoked? .... Yes No

(d) Has any surety company paid out any funds on your coverage? .... Yes No

If answer to either (b), (c) or (d) is "yes", attach details including name of surety company.

2. Have you ever been a member of any stock exchange, commodity exchange, or registered association of security or commodity brokers, dealers, investment bankers or investment advisors? .... Yes No

If "yes", give name(s) and dates.

3. (a) Have you ever been suspended, expelled or otherwise disciplined by any regulatory body or by any such exchange or association; or ever been denied membership therein; or ever withdrawn your application for such membership? .... Yes No

(b) Have you ever been associated with any organization, as a director, controlling stockholder, partner, officer, employee or other representative of a broker-dealer which has been, or a principal of which has been, suspended or expelled from any such exchange or registered association, or was denied membership therein, or withdrawn an application for membership; or whose registration as a broker-dealer with the S.E.C. or, any State or agency has been denied, suspended or revoked? .... Yes No

(c) Has any permanent or temporary injunction ever been entered against you? .... Yes No

(d) Has any corporation, firm, or association, with which you were associated, been enjoined during the period of your association? .... Yes No

(e) If answer to question 3 (a), (b), (c), or (d) is "yes", attach details including any finding that you were a cause of any disciplinary action or had violated any law. ....

4. In your previous business connections or employment in any capacity, have transactions under your attention ever been the subject of complaint or legal proceedings? .... Yes No

If "yes", give names and details.

5. Have you ever been convicted of a felony of any kind, or of a misdemeanor except minor traffic offenses? .... Yes No

If "yes", attach details.

6. Have you ever been known personally by any other name, used an alias, or have you ever conducted business or carried brokerage or bank accounts in any other name than that shown above? .... Yes No

If "yes", give details and dates of use.

I hereby certify that I have read and understood the foregoing statements and that each of my responses thereto is true and complete. I authorize my employer, if I am hired, to make available to any prospective employer, or to any Federal, State or Municipal agency, any information it may have concerning me, and I hereby release my employer, if I am hired, from any and all liability of whatsoever nature by reason of furnishing such information.

I authorize all persons, schools, companies, corporations, credit bureaus and law enforcement agencies to supply any information concerning my background, and release them from any liability and responsibility arising from their doing so.

I understand further that any misrepresentation or omission of facts is sufficient cause for cancellation of this application or separation from the company's service if I am employed.

_____   _____
(Signature of Applicant)   (Date)

Approved_____
(Authorized Officer)   11—01—12

numbers for certifications, such as those for nurses, pilots, engineers, or teachers, and your birth certificate; e) extra copies of your résumé or samples of your work (if you are a writer, designer, or artist). Granted, the latter may not be applicable to the application form, but each is a special consideration for you.

Maturation. An employer seeks a mature, confident employee. In Chapter One you will recall reading the examples of very poor letters of application. Such weaknesses are just as common in the application forms completed by hopeful candidates. We are confident that you, as an intelligent applicant, will read each question or item *carefully* and that you will not even write your name until you have determined, "Yes, it *does* go in that blank" and, "Yes, my last name is requested first. . . ." Ink is difficult to erase. If you can, request permission to take a complex application form home and then prepare it carefully, typing the final form.

Maturity is shown in the manner in which you request the application form. When you are present in the office, thank the person giving it to you. The manner with which you cross to an assigned place to complete the form, the poise and posture maintained while completing it, and the care in which you return it to the employer may all be observed. We urge you to read every item twice to be certain you are providing the required information. Did the form request that you "write" your name or did it ask you to "print" it? Does the required information go above or below the line? Follow instructions carefully. If an item does not pertain to your case, omit it or else write "n/a" (not-applicable) in the blank. Sometimes simply drawing a brief dash through the space provided will show that you have considered that item.

A Special Challenge. We concur with any applicant who does not enjoy completing a question which states: "In the space provided below, write a brief personal biography in 100 words or less," or ". . . write the major events or persons which have influenced your life," or ". . . write your major achievements or goals in 100 words or less," or ". . . write your personal philosophy of education in 100 words or less." If you are faced with such an item, prepare it carefully to reflect your maturity and your ability to think and write. Woe unto the applicant who writes: "I was born, raised, . . . and died." Frequently, a high school graduate or a student requesting entrance into a graduate program will also face such a challenge. The major purposes of such questions are to check your maturity, to identify important information, and to determine whether you use correct written expression. Review some of the better letters of application provided in Chapter One and some of the "experience" descriptions in Chapter Two for some ideas about how to focus your paragraph. Write your paragraph on other paper first and then revise it before transferring your thoughts to the application form.

A Look at the Sample Applications. The two sample applications are significantly different: The one for "Three Oaks Restaurant" is brief and simple; the longer, "second form," is quite complex. The first is for a beginning employee such as a waitress. The second is for a key employee with a brokerage firm. Remember, any question must be *bona fide* and be directly relevant to the position for which you are being considered. Some current forms contain statements such as:

The Civil Rights Act of 1964 prohibits discrimination in employment practice because of race, color, religion, sex, or national origin. Public Law 90-202 prohibits discrimination on the basis of age with respect to individuals who are at least 40 but less than 65 years of age. In addition the laws of this state prohibit discrimination because of marital status and against the handicapped as well as the utilization of credit data. [This description was developed specifically for this chapter.]

In the one-page application for "Three Oaks," the questions relating to health are directly applicable to any applicant seeking a position as a waitress or chef. Perhaps the question relevant to marital status is not job related and could be omitted. Our reaction is that you should use your good judgment regarding any question which is personal and does not seem to relate directly to the position. We would answer such questions unless they were obviously in poor taste or totally unrelated to us. We find nothing in the "Three Oaks" application which should be offensive or difficult to answer. The long form, on which no company name is provided, offers a different challenge.

In the second example, many questions are quite probing and personal. However, since this application form is obviously for a concern which handles extensive amounts of monies, deals with securities, and with the federal government, most questions can be defended as *bona fide* (i.e., directly related to requirements for the position). After reading the total application form, it becomes predictable that the applicant is going to have an extensive search conducted regarding his or her background prior to being given a position of significant responsibility.

The last sheet of this form is highly specific. Review it in order to gain an insight into what types of questions you might expect when applying for a senior position. Of course, you will need to relate the questions or rephrase them to fit the type of position you are seeking. In addition, you will need to consider which special questions might be more relevant to your line of endeavor. In conclusion, review the serious implications of the last three paragraphs you are required to sign. Any perjury in completing this form would be quite serious, probably calling for immediate dismissal. Such an action could affect your future career potential seriously.

SPECIAL PROBLEMS IN EMPLOYMENT INTERVIEWS

Special problems include the following:

Getting a Job

Isn't it who you know, not what you know? The old question about the importance of having good contacts (or "good friends in high places") is asked repeatedly when it comes to getting jobs. Certainly many jobs, if not a vast majority of jobs, are awarded because "someone knew someone who knew someone." This may be particularly true of part-time jobs where "nepotism" (the hiring of one's family) seems particularly pervasive.

There are three influences that seem to discourage such practices, however: (1) Some companies have anti-nepotism policies. (2) Some managers look askance at the practice of hiring friends for fear of collusion, cliquishness, and general personnel problems. (3) Affirmative Action influences to provide equal employment opportunities have encouraged employers to employ persons of races, creeds, cultures, sex, circumstances, and backgrounds different from those of the vast majority of their employees.

Afraid to Participate

What do I do about my fear, lack of confidence, or reticence about self-disclosure when it comes time for an interview? There are many notions about how to overcome fear that have little basis in reality. For many people, confidence in public speech situations builds slowly, and then they may feel uncomfortable when it comes to speaking about themselves (self-disclosure). This is a very real problem and a great handicap for many.

Enrolling in a speech course or a Dale Carnegie program will undoubtedly force one to confront one's fear of speaking in public. Many speech communication teachers and coaches have exercises, group activities, and other means of gradually slipping students into positions where they can speak with confidence.

Weekend workshops in speech, interpersonal communication, and interviewing are becoming more available through management associations, company employee enrichment programs, and college and university continuing education departments. Enroll in a course. Contact a speech communication department.

Wearing Apparel

What should I wear? Should a female job applicant wear pants (or a pants suit) to an employment interview?

The answer to this question is simple—"Wear what is appropriate!" The trouble is that the answer is too simple. What does "appropriate" mean? Doesn't it mean various things and depend upon individual taste and judgment? Obviously, it does. Therefore, we might say to someone, "Wear what *you* think is right, what makes you feel comfortable. Pick out something that makes you feel confident." That advice might help the feelings of the applicant, but it may give a bad impression to those who have to view the applicant.

Certainly wearing apparel—or lack of it (short skirts, plunging necklines, tight pants)—which is extreme or calls attention to itself would not be appropriate. It might be eye-catching and "popular" but certainly not appropriate. The same is true for grooming (unusual hairstyle, heavily laid on or bizarre cosmetics) which may make an impression—but the wrong impression.

A good rule of thumb may be to dress in a style which would seem appropriate to the majority of the employees—to wear what they would wear if invited to a very important meeting by the manager. If they did not wear their uniforms, shop or lab clothes, what would *they* consider appropriate? If in doubt, dress on the conservative side.

Trick Questions

How should I handle trick, embarrassing, or illegal questions?

One viable alternative in retortmanship, often overlooked by inexperienced interviewees, is simply to decline to answer a question. If you feel a question is inappropriate to you, politely state: "I don't think I should answer that question or discuss that topic at this time."

Another way of putting it is to smile and reply, "I'm not quite prepared to answer that particular question but I might tell you that my tentative thinking on the matter is. . . ."

You could, of course, say bluntly, "Well, that is not a very good question, is it?" or "That question is too personal for a business interview," or "I'd rather not comment on that matter because the answer might entail information which could be prejudicial."

Be careful not to alienate, however. Try to remain composed and pleasant even if the interviewer becomes tense and obnoxious. After all, you may find that this is merely a test to see how you handle yourself in the face of tricky, embarrassing, or illegal questions.

Illegal Questions

What are some of the tricky or illegal questions that might be asked in employment interviews?

There are many questions that follow the pattern of the old classic question, "Have you stopped beating your mother yet?"

Whether you answer "yes" or "no," you are guilty of saying something wrong. The only answer is a careful explanation that gets you out of the trap.

Another of these tricky questions is: "Are you a loner or a joiner?" The implication is that either you can get along in a working relationship with others or you can't. Either you are independent and self-motivated or you are not.

Don't let yourself get hung up on these tricky, either-or questions. Explain the alternatives. Demonstrate how you can be both loner *and* joiner.

Illegal questions, which show up more obviously on application forms, are questions which demand information regarding your race, creed, political affiliations, club memberships, and so forth. Many questions of this type violate the spirit of the equal opportunity employment policy as well as state and federal laws barring discrimination.

Ineptness

How do you deal with an inept interviewer?

Don't scold, ridicule, or try to retrain the inept interviewer. Frequently our students will engage in interviews in the community and come back with stories describing their experiences. "Was he bad! He had no idea how to conduct an interview. He was so incompetent that after our interview was all over, I told him, 'Look, first of all, don't try to conduct an interview in here with all these interruptions! What you have got to learn to understand is that the purpose of an interview is. . . .'"

Granted, many interviewers could benefit from training sessions; but it is not *your* job, or the time, or the place to train your interviewer. Your responsibility is to make *your* interview a success, not to train the interviewer for future encounters with others.

If an interviewer "freezes" or gets "bogged down," don't get tense or nervous about it. Take your time. Provide some breathing space—perhaps by offering a copy of your résumé for the interviewer to look over while gaining some composure. If nothing constructive happens for a long period of time, offer some initiative by posing a question yourself—to yourself. You might say, for example, "You might wonder what experience I've had." Then go on to provide an account of your experiences, and so forth.

Notetaking and Recording

Should I record or take notes during an interview? Answers to this question frequently run the complete gamut from "No, don't take any!" to "Yes, take as many as you can!"

The answer probably lies somewhere in between. You do not want to impair your visual contact with your interviewer or impede the free flow of questions and dialogue. Some interviewers might share information with you if they were certain it would *not* be recorded. That is why making audio tape recordings of interviews is taboo and why taking notes on everything is not a good idea.

If in doubt, ask the interviewer: "Is this something I should be taking notes about?" or "Do you mind if I jot these facts down?" Some interviewers will want you to jot down items and be impressed if you do so efficiently and unobtrusively.

Whether you take notes or not, you should be prepared (with pen and pad) to do so.

"How Long Must I Wait?"

This question is often asked by persons who have applied for a job, been interviewed, and then have been told by the employer, "We will notify you." So you wait and you wait and you wonder.

Some jobs in the work force are filled rather rapidly. You may hear from your interviewer in a month or even in a week. Other jobs, especially high level management positions, may not be filled for six to eight months. We have known of positions which were prematurely advertised only to be frozen by a lack of funds. A year or two later, the "budget line" of this position was thawed out and the interviews were again resumed.

A significant point is that if you occupy a high position, or have recently resigned from one, prepare to assess your finances. To find a comparable (especially high-level management) position or a better one, you may need as much as one year's time and two years' savings to tide you over.

Our advice is:

1. Study your finances (mortgage, interest payments, and so forth).
2. Budget well (consider unemployment or other sources of income such as working spouse).
3. Have patience and don't panic.
4. Don't accept the first position that comes along unless it's the one you really want.
5. Continue your search for other comparable positions.
6. Prepare your family for possible vicissitudes.

"What If I Have Two or More Job Considerations or Offers?"

If you have been offered a position while another position is pending, you have a decision to make. You may, in such an instance, call the interviewer on the telephone. Ask if you are still being considered for the first position. Explain that you have been offered another opportunity and that you must make a decision. (You are not obligated to reveal the source or the terms and conditions.) Then wait for the interviewer's response. Sometimes the interviewer will make the decision for you. Do not rely on this, however. You must make your own decision. If you decide to accept the second position, tell your first potential employer so.

Consider the position of the employer. He is in a bind, too. For example, recently we were attempting to fill a position and had announced an August 15 deadline for the acceptance of applications. On August 10, one of the candidates called to inform us that he had another offer but preferred our position. "What should I do?" he asked. We explained that we had an obligation to accept any applications that we received on or before August 15. "But where do I stand," he persisted, "Does my application look better than most? Are you going to be forced to hire a minority-type person?"

This line of questioning is out of order. One can understand and sympathize with the "jobless candidate." However, the questions being raised are private business. For us to make a "prejudgment" on this candidate's opportunities would be both prejudicial and unethical. Don't be pushy with employers!

Questions of Salary

"How should I bring up the question of salary?" Employers and interviewers disagree about how the question of salary should be handled. Our experience reveals that any applicant would be wise to know a salary range and to have a firm idea as to salary requirements.

WHEN SHOULD THE QUESTION OF SALARY BE RAISED?

Some interviewers believe that the applicant should introduce this question. Our research does not support this position, nor does sound common sense. It is much more realistic to expect the interviewer to introduce the subject of salary since he is more relaxed and is in control of the interview situation. We do suggest that, unless absolutely necessary, or unless requested, you avoid stating salary demands in your letter of application. In most cases this question should be discussed in the interview. Do be prepared and don't get caught unprepared for such an important question. "What salary do you anticipate?" "Sir, I have discussed this question with others in the field; and, with my experience, I would consider a salary between $_____ and $_____ to be a fair range. Frankly, I am confident that I should be worth $_____ to Winston Electronics."

Frequently, we are asked by members of the military who are changing careers (1) what salary to expect, or (2) what to do when an employer tells them that they do not need as high a salary since they have their military retirement pay.

The first question can apply to anyone. If you have no idea as to an appropriate salary, we would recommend that you talk with others already employed in that field who are experienced and qualified to recommend a salary range for you based upon your level of experience and as compared with others. It is imperative that you do not "price" yourself too low; but it is also necessary that you are realistic regarding an adequate salary. Remember, there may be equally important considerations: Significant fringe benefits, training opportunities which might mean a higher salary in the long run, growth potential of a company, promotional opportunities, stock sharing, and commissions are also salary alternatives. You must consider the total "salary package" for a realistic evaluation of possible earnings.

The second question regarding the military retiree or any other person similarly changing careers is unfortunate. Too often, it does happen that an employer will attempt to hire a person far below his or her worth. Our advice is to speak frankly and openly and inform the interviewer that you expect to be paid what you are worth and that such an approach is unethical. In fact, neither of us would want to work for that employer since we could not respect such tactics. We believe strongly that the vast majority of employers would be appalled at such a practice. A respectable company wants employees who are content in their work and who are productive and dedicated to the company. No employer in his right mind wants to risk hiring unhappy employees.

REFERENCES

"Whom should I ask for a reference?" The use of references is adequately covered in Chapter Two. The significant problem you need to consider here is the selection of your references. Having read several hundreds of reference letters, we assure you that the *vast* majority are not really useful and that nearly all are viewed with suspicion. Most applicants have a variety of experiences. The high school or college graduate has had teachers of academic subjects, extra-curricular activities, advisors of organizations, or experience of a limited nature in the world of work. The wise applicant will select references who can provide insights into numerous aspects of his abilities. The teacher could point up his ability to write, to do quality academic work, to speak effectively; or he might stress his potential for advanced responsibilities or education as well as his insights into maturity and personality. The activity or organizational advisor can provide insights as to the applicant's social adaptability, his ability to get along with his peers, or his ability to lead. A former employer might provide insights into the applicant's ability to assume responsibility; his reliability, punctuality, and ability to work with others; his ease in meeting the public; or the quality of the work he performed.

It is our recommendation that any applicant select references who *know* the quality of his work and who can write wisely regarding future potential. We also recommend that you select references who can present the broad spectrum of your abilities and assets.

The wise applicant will also avoid using close friends who do not know the quality of his work. "I know Bill and his family well and can assure you that they are outstanding in every way." Sorry, but this will not get you the job. It might if the writer were a Nobel prize winner, but even then we doubt it. It may even be to your advantage to provide anyone you select with the job description—if one has been given to you. This way, your references will be able to write specifically to the criteria required. If care is not exercised in the selection of your references, you, too, might receive one of the following types of references—all of which are true.

A full Colonel (male) writing for a Major (female): "You have it upon my word of honor, she is truly outstanding in or out of uniform."

College professor writing for a student: "His work is not too bad and he should be able to perform in some useful capacity."

Manager writing for a friend (also a manager): "I know of no one whose loss to our company would be felt as greatly among those who have had the rare opportunity to see George's work."

Well known *name* in the field for person (candidate for college presidency) whom he has not known in four years: "I knew Dr. Smalley four or five years ago in a casual manner. As far as I know, he was building a good reputation at that time. Since 1972 I have only seen him for a few minutes at a convention. It would be my recommendation that you rely upon his immediate superiors or colleagues for any indepth comments."

It is truly important that you select your references with great care. Usually, friends appear as friends; ministers as ministers; and well known names (who do not know you well) as average—to your detriment. A few of the better letters we have read have come from unexpected sources: A subordinate wrote a superb letter about his "boss's" abilities and of the workers' respect for him; a student wrote an extraordinarily outstanding letter for a college professor attesting to his ability to teach, to inspire, and to help students; a major customer wrote an excellent letter confirming a salesman's ability to sell, service, and handle complaints, to convey new ideas to his company (writer needed new products), to offer suggestions which helped the customer increase his own sales—the letter also contained comments about his personality, his excellent follow-up, and his fairness to his competitors' products.

Remember, often an employer will not only read the letter of recommendation but will follow up with a phone call to the reference. This is especially true with experienced applicants seeking higher level positions. Will your references stand the test of such an in-depth call? If so, you have chosen wisely and you should be in excellent position to land that new opportunity.

ONE FINAL OPPORTUNITY— THE THANK YOU LETTER

In a survey of well over a thousand letters of application and their accompanying files, the authors found exactly ONE letter of thank you! This is unbelievable. There can be no question that good manners are always in order. If you receive a response to your letter—good or disappointing—write a brief thank you. If you are granted an interview, write a brief thank you. If you receive the position, write a thank you. We are confident that an applicant who does take this little extra effort will be gaining an edge over competition who do not. As a minimum, it provides you with the opportunity to place your name in a favorable light before the interviewer one more time. We have one example where an applicant wrote a thank you after being told there was no opening. A few days later he was requested to come for an interview by the same source. If you have enjoyed unusual courtesy such as dinner (either out or in a home), a thank you is absolutely in order. Remember, if a spouse of the interviewer has been generous to you, the thank you is also in order.

A FINAL WORD OF ADVICE

After each interview, keep a record of questions and of your assessment of the interview. In addition, once you have gained your position, KEEP your records in a file. A résumé which has been carefully prepared and which has proven successful is worth reviewing at some later date should you be requested to apply for another position. Often an outstanding manager is requested to "throw his hat" in the ring with minimum notice. A well-prepared résumé in a file is an asset in meeting a rushed deadline. With our current Affirmative Action laws, it is even more important that you be prepared to prove yourself the best qualified applicant. We would even suggest that your file contain all correspondence which you received for future reference.

Now that you have read this work, we urge you to review it, study possible potential positions, prepare your résumé, research the company, and plan for the interview with confidence. It is our mutual goal that this work has contributed to helping each reader "to become all he or she is capable of becoming."

Additional Résumés for Study

The reader is urged to review the appropriate description provided below before studying each résumé.

Sharon S. LeClair. This is a well written résumé for a young, inexperienced applicant. Note how Ms. LeClair's minimal experience is delineated according to the positions held.

Bonnie Lee Wiley. Ms. Wiley's résumé is also well written. Note the short, personal paragraph following her experience and her listing of her honors and activities.

Janice L. Nelson. Ms. Nelson represents a young, educated applicant with four years military experience. Résumé could be improved by listing experience before education and by highlighting her experience more.

John Russell. An excellent résumé of a highly experienced manager. Note his clear statement of his objective and the brief summary of his qualifications at the beginning. A good example of the functional style of organization. For persons having technical education, this résumé provides a good model for careful review.

Francis N. Carson. A very good example of a one-page résumé for a highly experienced person. Note the focus on functions.

Douglas V. Fernetti. This résumé depicts a successful journeyman/foreman desiring to change locations for family reasons. While such a résumé is "correct," it would be preferable to write just the letter of application, which could include all vital information. Personal reasons might better be left for the interview.

Jonathan Douglas. The résumé of a highly experienced command pilot/manager completing one career and desiring to change to industry. It would be stronger if experience came first and education second. Note that it also contains too many specifics and is too long.

William H. Nelson. Résumé of an experienced officer in management area who was retrenched ("riffed") from military service. Note the inclusion of extensive data. This is usually "too much." Honors might be left for the interview.

Alexander B. Castle. A senior non-commissioned officer changing careers after more than twenty years' service within one organization. This résumé illustrates how persons with long experience with one organization can summarize their experiences in stages of progression. This résumé is also much too long and should be edited.

Dr. Harold C. Grattan. This résumé represents a highly experienced college educator/administrator desiring to relocate. This unusually long, comprehensive résumé is expected by members of search committees, although a shorter one could be equally effective. This résumé is included to illustrate the broad types of information which might be considered within the education field.

R E S U M E

Sharon S. LeClair

PERSONAL DATA

Address: Box 751
         Kingston, New York 12980
Telephone: 914 791-7565
Date of Birth: May 22, 1950

Height: 5' 4"
Weight: 115 lbs.
Health: Excellent
Marital Status: Single

EDUCATIONAL RECORD

1963 - 1967 Kingston Kennedy High School, Kingston, New York. Regents'
              Diploma 1964.
1968 - 1972 Covington College, Covington, New York. Graduated with a
              B.S. Degree in Education. Major: Speech Pathology
              Minor: Science Academic Standing: upper 1/4th with B avg.

EMPLOYMENT RECORD

Student Teaching -- Student teaching was under the supervision of Mr. James
      Simmons, Science Teacher, Democracy, New York. 15 weeks in 1972.

Nurses Aide -- Kingston General Hospital, Kingston, New York. Served for
      four summers assisting nurses with preparing beds, meals, and other
      basic services. Earnings were used to defray one-half college costs.

Waitress -- Covington Inn, Covington, New York. A part time position
      during 1971 and 1972 to help defray college expenses.

EXTRACURRICULAR ACTIVITIES

Am an active member of Sigma Alpha Eta, American Speech and Hearing Assoc.
Honorary, and am a volunteer Speech Clinician for two children unable
to attend regular classes. Am also an editor for college newspaper
and active in student government. Serve as a tutor for students
in our Equal Opportunity Program.

LEISURE TIME ACTIVITY

Am an avid reader and do some free lance articles. Also enjoy gourmet cooking
(French and Chinese), skiing, camping, and music.

CERTIFICATES AND SPECIAL ASSETS

Received Permanent Teaching Certificate, State of New York, June, 1976.
Also hold Clinical Certification in Pathology, American Speech and Hearing Assoc.
Have fluent reading and writing knowledge of both English and French.

REFERENCES

Credentials are on file with: Office of Career Planning and Placement
                        Covington College
                        Covington, New York 12790

Sharon S. LeClair—A young, inexperienced applicant in the education field.

BONNIE LEE WILEY
66 North 9th Avenue
Stillwater, Oklahoma 74074

Phone: 918 761-3333

EDUCATION: 1969-73 Stillwater High School, Stillwater, Oklahoma 74075
Diploma 1973. Business curriculum.

1973-75 Tulsa Business Institute, Tulsa, Oklahoma 74111
AA Degree 1975. Major: Secretarial Science and Office
Management.

EXPERIENCE:

1974-75 Mr. Nelson A. Keebler, Certified Public Accountant and
Attorney-at-Law, 616 Main Street, Tulsa, Oklahoma.
Position: Served part-time (twenty hours per week) as
personal secretary. Duties included typing, correspondence, briefs and income tax returns as well as
general filing.

1971-74 Did miscellaneous odd jobs during the school year. During the summers 1971, 72, and 73, worked at the Wharf
Restaurant, Stillwater, Oklahoma, as a hostess.

Consider my major attributes to be my competency in
typing and shorthand, reliability, and my ability to
communicate with the public.

HONORS: Elected vice president (1972) and president (1973) of
my class at Stillwater High School, member of the National Honor Society (1972-73), Recipient of the Edna
North Award for "Outstanding Business Major".

ACTIVITIES: Stillwater High School --
    Member of the Student Council 1970-73 (President, '73)
    Business Club (President, 1972)
    Editor, Cardinal Points (school paper), 1972-73
Tulsa Institute:
    Secretarial Science Club (vice-president 1975)
    President's Advisory Committee (1975)
Community:
    Have served as a reader for hospital patients,
    active in fund raising activities, and a member
    of the First Baptist Church. Also enjoy reading,
    camping, and a variety of sports.

PERSONAL: Born: January 5, 1952 Height: 5'5" Weight: 128 lbs.

REFERENCES: References are available upon request.

**Bonnie Lee Wiley—A young, minimally experienced applicant in secretarial
science and office management.**

<u>R E S U M E</u>

Janice L. Nelson
77 MacDonough Street
Plattsburgh, New York 12901
Telephone: 565-5000
(after 4:30 561-3000)

Height: 5' 5"
Weight: 105 lb.
Date of Birth: June 4, 1948
Single

EDUCATION:

Formal: 1972 Matriculation in Administrative Science degree
               program with an emphasis in accounting at the
               State University of New York, Plattsburgh, New
               York. Bachelor of Science degree anticipated
               in June, 1974.

         1971 Twelve credit hours at Clinton Community College,
               Plattsburgh, New York consisting of Business Law
               I and II, Criminal Justice and Personnel Manage-
               ment.

         1970 B.S. Ed. degree from Berry State College, Berry,
               Pennsylvania. Professional teaching certificate
               in mathematics awarded by Commonwealth of Penn-
               sylvania.

         1966 Governors High School, Pittsburgh, Pennsylvania,
               Diploma in College Preparatory Curriculum.

Technical: 1972 Honor Graduate of Legal Services Specialist School,
                  Keesler Air Force Base, Mississippi. Specialized
                  training received in claims adjudication, investi-
                  gating, court reporting and military justice.

                  Legal Specialist/Technician course of the United
                  States Air Force Extension Course Institute.

            1971 Apprentice Administration Specialist course of the
                  U.S.A.F. Extension Course Institute.

                  U.S.A.F. Documentation Management Course.

                  U.S.A.F. Equipment Custodian Course.

            1970 Ground Radio Operator Technical School, Keesler
                  Air Force Base, Mississippi. Specialized training
                  received in radio voice procedures and typewriting.

Janice L. Nelson—A young, educated applicant with four years military
experience.

EXPERIENCE:

    1972 Non-commissioned officer in charge of claims at Plattsburgh
          Air Force Base, New York.

    1971 Claims examiner, Plattsburgh Air Force Base, New York.

    1970 Documentation Clerk of the Tactical Communications Branch,
          Plattsburgh Air Force Base, New York.

    1960-1969 Miscellaneous employment: Quality control and inspector
          at Pittsburgh-Corning Corporation, Port Allegany, Pennsylvania;
          stock clerk and typist for Smethport Auto Parts, Smethport,
          Pennsylvania.

PROFESSIONAL AFFILIATIONS:

    National Council of Teachers of Mathematics and Lambda Gamma Sigma
    (honorary mathematics fraternity).

HONORS:

    Educational Vice-President of the Adirondack Junior League Club in
    1971. Named to Dean's List four times at State College, Berry,
    Pennsylvania.

COMMUNITY SERVICE:

    Plattsburgh Air Force Base, New York: Fifth grade Sunday School
    teacher, counselor for the Protestant Youth of the Chapel, Children's
    Chapel Service song leader, director of youth singing group "The
    Messengers" and assistant Babe Ruth League baseball coach.

ACTIVITIES:

    College: Student Senate, mixed chorus, golf, bowling, tutor of
            high school mathematics.

    Air Force: Keesler Air Force Base Chorus, golf and tennis.

REFERENCES:

    References are available on request from:

            Director of Placement
            State College
            Berry, Pennsylvania   16213

R E S U M E

JOHN RUSSELL
701 South 61st Street
Shreveport, Louisiana 71150
Telephone:
    Home (318) 834-8161
    Office (318) 394-4692/4693

Height: 5'9"
Weight: 170 lbs.
Birthdate: June 18, 1932
Married: Wife, Betty
Daughters: Harriet (Married)
           Susan (18 yrs.)

OBJECTIVE

Senior management position in financial or administrative areas of corporate enterprise.

SUMMARY OF QUALIFICATIONS

Advanced degree and experience in all areas of financial management. Extensive experience in managing and working with people. Qualified in the full spectrum of business management: planning, budgeting, environmental considerations, information plans, analysis and electronic data processing. Dedication to the organization and to work effort and ability to motivate personnel are my most significant personal attributes.

EXPERIENCE

Comptroller/ Management

1972 - Present. UNITED STATES AIR FORCE, Air Command, AFB, Louisiana. Chief, Management Information Division (Colonel): Responsible for developing and maintaining the management system used in the headquarters and at fifteen other Air Force bases. Also direct an innovative budget process for the command in the distribution and control of a 600 million dollar budget. Additional duties include supervising financial management studies and analyses to include costing, budgeting, trend analysis and forecasting.

Administration

1955 - 1957 and 1959 - 1972. UNITED STATES AIR FORCE. During these periods responsibilities included managing base level plans function, intelligence operations, command and control functions, advisor to battle staff, combat crew training instructor, standardization evaluator and aircrew member. Performed as primary navigator on over fifteen different Air Force aircraft.

Audit

1957 - 1959. UNITED STATES TREASURY DEPARTMENT, INTERNAL REVENUE SERVICE, Washington, D.C. Performed complete federal tax liability audits of business enterprises for approximately one-fifth the state of Kentucky. Audit candidate selection, schedules, techniques and methods were my responsibility. Taxpayer assistance and office management were also primary functions.

Banking

1949 - 1951. COMMERCIAL BANK, Peoria, Illinois. After high school and prior to entering college I worked in the main office of a major Peoria bank. Positions included a variety of banking duties including paying and receiving teller.

John Russell—A senior manager who has completed a distinguished military career and desires to enter a senior management position.

EDUCATION
Formal

KANSAS UNIVERSITY, Morgan, Kansas. Masters in Business Administration, 1967. MAJOR: Business Management with special emphasis in accounting and economics.

UNIVERSITY OF KENTUCKY, Lexington, Kentucky. Bachelor of Science, 1959; MAJOR: Accounting; MINOR: Personnel Management

Professional

Other than my eighteen month professional Navigator's School in 1955, I have attended over ten professional schools. The following are most significant:

ARMED FORCES POSTGRADUATE SCHOOL, Monterey, California, 1973 Fifty day training program in concepts, principles and methods of defense management with emphasis on analytical aspects of management, economics and quantitative analysis.

AIR UNIVERSITY INSTITUTE FOR PROFESSIONAL DEVELOPMENT, Maxwell AFB, Alabama, 1972. Sixty day (2100 class hours) "Professional Military Comptroller Course" examining the roll of the Comptroller as financial advisor; the economic, social and political environment which influences decision making processes, and the application of management information systems in meeting goals and objectives.

MILITARY MANAGEMENT ENGINEERING TRAINING AGENCY, Little Rock, Arkansas, 1973. Twenty days training in workshops and seminars designed to present, search out and discuss the most current best business practices. Also concerned with organizational design, development, theories, concepts and applications.

RECOGNITION

Have been privileged to receive five commendations for outstanding performance of financial and managerial responsibilities such as: "...highly innovative planning resulting in over $3,000,000 in savings". Also a member of Phi Kappa Delta.

PERSONAL
INTERESTS

Memberships include Masonic Lodge, Scottish Rite, Shriner and several military organizations of similar purpose. Hobbies include golf, tennis, boating and traveling.

<u>R E S U M E</u>

Francis N. Carson
801 Cornelia
Bonaire, California 95655
Phone: 916 723-4455
        or 723-7275 after 6:00pm

Born: April 12, 1930
Height: 5'10" Weight: 185
Health: Excellent
Married: Joan
Children: David (18), Mary (16)

OBJECTIVE: Desire a senior management position which utilizes a proven
            background in mechanical engineering and administration.

EDUCATION:
            College of the City of Los Angeles, B.S. 1952
                Major -- Mechanical Engineering   Minor -- Civil Engineering
            Polytechnic Institute of Technology, M.S. 1973
                Major -- Industrial Engineering (completed during evenings)

GENERAL BACKGROUND:
            Twenty-four years experience with the following:

<u>CHIEF ENGINEER</u>   Bonaire, California
                         1956 to Present.

<u>PROJECT ENGINEER</u>   State Highway Department, New York
                         1954-1956.

<u>SYSTEMS ENGINEER</u>   U. S. Army Material Area, Indianapolis, Ind.
                         1952-1954.

<u>ADMINISTRATION & SUPERVISION</u> -- Over-all supervision of engineering staffs
        for the City of Bonaire. Responsible for the overall hiring,
        training, evaluation, and supervision of over 1,000 personnel.
        Fully knowledgeable of all aspects of employee supervision to in-
        clude contract negotiations, affirmative action laws, and employee
        motivation. Direct administration of all city engineering prob-
        lems and projects to include evaluation of new building plans,
        environmental impact studies, design and development of city
        projects such as streets and bridges as well as sanitary disposal
        plant construction. Also responsible for a multi-million dollar
        budget and payroll as well as for budgeting, contracts, scheduling,
        programs, department coordination, estimating, procurement, and
        audits. Work with a broad cross-section of people ranging from
        local citizens to city, state and federal agencies.

<u>DESIGN AND DEVELOPMENT</u> -- Designed and developed both automatic and
        special machines, instrumentation systems, hydraulics, pneumatics,
        and tooling. Have cooperated in the design and development of
        major engineering projects ranging from underriver tunnels, to
        bridges, to high rise structures. Have also done major Research.

<u>PROFESSIONAL AFFILIATION</u> -- Member of the American Society of
        Mechanical Engineers.

LICENSE: Professional Engineer (California and Indiana)

REFERENCES: Furnished on request.

**Francis N. Carson—An experienced manager/mechanical and civil engineer
seeking a new career opportunity.**

DOUGLAS V. FERNETTI

Address: 636 Rugar Street
          Joliet, Illinois
          60451
Phone: 309 876-0023

Date of Birth: June 5, 1951
Height: 6' Weight: 195 lbs.
Health: Excellent
Married: Helen   Son: Jim (2)

EXPERIENCE

1968 to 1973: Joliet Bridge and Girder Company, Joliet, Illinois.
Began as an apprentice and became accomplished journeyman
Pattern Maker.

1973 to Present: Joliet Bridge and Girder Company, Joliet, Illinois.
Promoted to Forman, Pattern Division. Responsibilities
include the supervision of fourteen personnel, maintaining
work schedules and making assignments, maintaining stock
inventories, and supervising two apprentices.

PERSONAL ACTIVITIES

From 1969 to 1973 attended evening school in order to
complete my high school education. Received H.S. Diploma
from the State of Illinois in 1973. Since 1973 have
attended evening classes at Joliet Community College.
Have completed eighteen semester hours credit with nine
hours in personnel management. Other activities include
regular church attendance, member of the Elks, and help
with Little League.

PERSONAL STATEMENT

Although I have been very happy at Joliet Bridge and Girder
and have had excellent opportunity, it is necessary that
I relocate my family due to my son's allergies. In this
respect, desire a position in the Southwest United States.
Am willing to consider a position as a pattern maker, tool
and die maker, or as a supervisor. My major attributes
are my reliability and loyalty to my company and my ability
to work with others.

REFERENCES

References are available upon request.

Douglas V. Fernetti—A successful journeyman/foreman.

R E S U M E

Johnathan Douglas
61 West Adirondack Lane
Bristol, New Hampshire 03222
Phone: 603-560-5594 (office)
        603-567-5212 (home)

Height: 6'0"
Weight: 185 lbs.
Birthdate: March 30, 1934
Married: Wife, Carolyn
Sons: Mike (15 yrs.)
       Greg (13 yrs.)

EDUCATION:

Formal:

Matriculation in the General Studies degree program at the State University of New York, College of Arts and Sciences, Plattsburgh, New York. Four concentrations of study include: Communication Arts, Mathematics, Computer Science, and Administrative Science. Bachelor of Arts degree anticipated in August, 1975.

Associate in Arts degree by the Board of Regents of the University of the State of New York, Albany, New York. Degree work completed in December, 1973. Major: Administrative Science.

Technical:

During my twenty years in the Air Force, I have attended over twenty service schools.

Some of the more significant professional military educational schools include:

1. PILOT TRAINING SCHOOLS, six months each, Graham Air Base, Florida and Williams Air Force Base, Arizona.
2. NAVIGATOR TRAINING SCHOOL, six month course at James Connelly Air Force Base, Texas.
3. AIR COMMAND AND STAFF COLLEGE, nine month program in senior management and international relations at Maxwell Air Force Base, Alabama.
4. SQUADRON OFFICERS SCHOOL, correspondence program evaluated for 6 semester hours credit completed through the United States Air Force Extension Course Institute.
5. CONCEPTS OF LEADERSHIP, Plattsburgh Air Force Base, a 36 hour seminar at PAFB taught by the State University of New York.

Experience:
Dec. 1970
to
Present

CHIEF, TRAINING DEVICES BRANCH, Plattsburgh Air Force Base, New York. Responsibilities include supervision of seventy-eight civilian and military personnel. Responsible for all aspects of ground training and budgeting. Managing the Utilization and maintenance of $35 million worth of Training Devices with an annual supply budget of $93 thousand.

Jonathan Douglas—The résumé of a command pilot/manager completing one career and desiring to change to industry.

TACTICAL SQUADRON FLIGHT COMMANDER, Plattsburgh Air Force Base, New York. Responsible for directing and supervising the activities of seven FB-111 Combat Crews to include evaluation of personnel.

UNIT STANDARDIZATION OFFICER, Nakom Phonom Royal Thai Air Force Base, Thailand. Responsible for the evaluation and upgrade program of seventy-five rescue helicopter crew members. Also, UNIT TRAINING OFFICER. Responsible for the proficiency flight training of seventy-five helicopter crew members.

Apr. 1966
to
Dec. 1969

COMBAT CREW TRAINING SCHOOL INSTRUCTOR PILOT, Grissom Air Force Base, Indiana. Responsible for aircrew training and evaluation of crew members transitioning to the supersonic B-58 aircraft.

Apr. 1956
to
Aug. 1964

SQUADRON AIRCRAFT COMMANDER, Schilling Air Force Base, Kansas. Responsible for maintaining crew proficiency plus performing flight leader duties on more than forty transoceanic flights.

SQUADRON COPILOT, Schilling Air Force Base, Kansas. Assisted Aircraft Commander and Navigator in performing combat crew duties. My additional duties included Squadron Scheduling and Ground Training Officer.

Aircraft:

My flying experience was acquired in the following aircraft, starting with the most recent: FB-111, T-29, HH-53, CH-3, HH-1, B-47, B-58, F-102, C-47, B-25, T-33, T-28, T-6 and PA-18. Almost all of my navigator experience has been in the T-29 aircraft. My flying experience totals over five thousand hours.

AWARDS:

Awards presented for meritorious and distinguished service include: Distinguished Graduate, Primary Pilot training; Air Force Commendation medal; Air Force Air Medal with two oak leaf clusters; the Distinguished Flying Cross; and, Dean's List at State University of New York (1973-1975).

COMMUNITY
SERVICE:

Boy Scouts of America, Committee Member, Troup 49, Peru, New York; Fifth and Sixth grade basketball coach, Randall Elementary School, Grissom Air Force Base, Indiana; Director and manager of fund drives including the Combined Federal Campaign; work with retarded children; and, civilian rescue work.

FRATERNAL
ORGANIZATIONS:

Bunker Hill Lodge Number 683, Free and Accepted Masons, Bunker Hill, Indiana. Ancient Accepted Scottish Rite, Valley of Fort Wayne, Indiana. Hadji Shrine Temple, Pensacola, Florida.

REFERENCES:

References are available upon request.

Resume of:
William H. Nelson

111A New York Avenue
Mountain Home AFB, Montana 59700
Phone: Home: 406-563-6000
Office: 406-565-0000

JOB
OBJECTIVES: A responsible and challenging position which utilizes a
background in management/administration of organizations
providing diverse goods and services. Desire a clear
opportunity to assume increasing responsibilities.

EDUCATION:
FORMAL
STATE UNIVERSITY OF ILLINOIS, ARLINGTON, ILLINOIS.
Master of Arts 1975; Major concentration in Public Adminis-
tration with minors in Personnel Administration and Manage-
ment. Also earned graduate credits with the University of
Alaska and Ball State University.

PROVIDENCE COLLEGE, Providence, Rhode Island.
Bachelor of Arts 1964; Majored in Economics.

SERVICE
AIR COMMAND AND STAFF COLLEGE, 1974, USAF Extension Course
Institute. Evaluated by the American Council of Education as equivalent to 12 graduate credits in Management
and International Relations.

SQUADRON OFFICERS SCHOOL, 1972, USAF Extension Course
Institute. Evaluated by the American Council of Education as equivalent to 9 credits in Management and Communications.

OFFICER TRAINING SCHOOL, 1964, San Antonio, Texas. A
three-month intensive training course in leadership, personnel management, human relations, international relations,
written and oral communication techniques. Upon graduation
received a commission as an Officer in the U.S. Air Force.

Also completed a Technical Representative of the Contracting
Officer Course, 1966, Denver, Colorado; Exchange Officer
Management Course, 1965, New York, NY; and a Commissary
Operations Course, 1964, Amarillo, Texas.

EXPERIENCE:
June 1971
to
Present
CHIEF, SERVICES DIVISION: As a Captain, responsible for a
workforce of up to 150 civilians and foreign national personnel and a staff of two Officers, four Officer grade
civilians and three senior Noncommissioned Officers. Direct
a major staff agency reporting to the Base Commander. Personnel responsibilities included selection, orientation,
training, supervision, evaluation, counselling, equal opportunity, affirmative action, labor-management relations and
terminations. Financial responsibilities include: budgeting, cash controls, inventories, equipment, vehicles, and
up to 15 buildings. Administratively responsible for security, documentation, classified materials, publications,

**William H. Nelson—Résumé of an experienced officer in management area
who was retrenched ("riffed") from military service.**

conservation of resources, planning, inspections, safety and manpower. Authorized grade level for this position was a Lt Colonel, equivalent to a GS-13/14.

January 1965
to
May 1971

EXCHANGE OFFICER (various bases): As a Captain with the Army and Air Force Exchange Service, Dallas, Texas, a profit oriented, nonappropriated instrumentality of the United States, directed the operation and management of up to 15 retail outlets, 14 food outlets, 2 mobile food outlets, 10 vending banks, 2 automotive service stations, supporting warehouses and administrative offices. Also administered up to 75 concession contracts. As Southern District Exchange Officer in Alaska, employed 497 civilians on three installations. Annual sales of $19 million represented 57 percent of the total Alaskan Exchange System sales. In Vietnam, with 38 U.S. and 41 Korean military; three U.S., 40 Phillipine, 10 Korean and 541 Vietnamese civilians operated facilities producing $3,300,000 monthly. In Texas, operated facilities on two installations with annual sales of $3,500,000. Generally, personnel responsibilities included recruitment, processing, bonding, orientation, development, suggestions, counselling, benefit administration, insurance, leave, employee-management relations, evaluations, budgeting and terminations. Represented the Exchange in grievance procedures. Contract administration included determining requirements, soliciting bids, awarding, writing contracts, insuring services/products met specifications and that cash transactions were properly recorded. This position was also graded as a Lt Colonel, GS-13/14 position.

HONORS:

Although having received several honors, the award of two Commendation Medals are considered the most significant. In 1971, the Award read in part, "Captain Nelson's outstanding professional skill, dynamic leadership and astute management ability contributed significantly to improved and more effective service...Despite high personnel turnover, merchandise shortages and declining customer population, Captain Nelson's initiative...aided in achieving an overall increase in sales and net profit by implementation of improved management technique." In 1976, "...the outstanding professional skill, initiative, tact, and knowledge demonstrated by Captain Nelson in identifying and solving the problems...have contributed immeasurably to the welfare of the personnel in the military community."

PERSONAL:

Born August 11, 1940, Andover, Massachusetts. Height: 5' 10", 160 lbs. Married 1965, two children, ages 8 and 4. Wife, Karen, graduated from the University of Maine and Mount Ida Junior College, majored in French. She also attended the University of Caen, Normandy, France, and studied German with the University of Maryland in Germany.

R E S U M E

Alexander B. Castle
3165 Millage Road
White Plains, NY 11793

Date of Birth: January 3, 1918
Heighth: 5'7" Weight 155
Health: Excellent
Marital Status: Married, Sandra

EDUCATION
Formal

Washington High School, Aaronsville, New York Diploma - 1936

Since graduation from high school, I have completed over three years of credit as evaluated by State University College of Arts and Science, New York. Major work was achieved as follows: over forty semester hours credit in humanities to include at least twelve hours in communications, over twenty-seven hours in management, as well as a four hundred fifty hour course in Foreign Trade through the University of the City of New York.

Professional

During my career with the United States Air Force, have attended numerous short courses and schools. The following are representative:

Non-Commissioned Officers Academy (1969) -- An intensive 12 week management program at the college level evaluated for six hours in management and three in international relations.

Management for Air Force Supervisors (1956 and 1958) -- Each is evaluated for college credit in management.

Concepts of Leadership and Management (1973) -- A thirty-six hour management seminar taught by the State University of New York, Plattsburgh, New York.

Spoken German, Rhein Main Air Base, Germany (1962) -- Fluent in both spoken and written German.

EXPERIENCE
Civilian

Assistant Traffic Manager, Export Department, Balfour Guthrie & Co., Ltd., New York. May 19, 1947 to July 31, 1950. Processed all necessary documentation for shipping merchandise overseas to foreign buyers to include customs declarations, counselor papers, and bills of lading. In meeting shipment schedules and deadlines, worked with several steamship companies as well as with railroads, motor freight, and air lines and mail. Also responsible for inspecting and determining disposition of damaged cargo.

Title Examiner, Home Title Guarantee Co., New York. August 1, 1950 to April 30, 1956. Abstracted information from public records to determine the validity and accuracy to insure clear titles. Also worked part time as a Real Estate Salesman. Was recalled to active military duty during this period.

Alexander B. Castle—A senior non-commissioned officer changing careers after more than twenty years service.

Title Searcher, Title Guarantee and Trust Co. January 10, 1937 to 15 July 1941. Served as abstracter of deeds, mortages, lis pendens, etc.

EXPERIENCE
Military

April 15, 1971 to present. Managerial Functions at five Air Bases, United States Air Force. During this period, was responsible for the orienting, training, supervision and evaluation of eight other managers (non-commissioned officers) and the several airmen serving these units. Specific responsibilities also included administration of Mission Development Branch as well as the Ground Training section. Responsible for coordinating and scheduling all training for tactical, non-tactical and staff crew members as well as maintaining all master schedules of flying and ground training and the documentation of all completed activities. Ancillary duties included assisting distinguished visitors and general officers and analyzing all personnel requests for air transportation to determine priorities. Hold Top Secret clearance.

September 8, 1958 to April 15, 1971. Managerial Functions as a non-commissioned officer at eleven Air Bases. Responsibilities and duties were similar to the above: Responsible for all personnel and for full utilization of these personnel and for the economy of operations. Significant additional duties included: responsible for entire Base Operations complex which included the Dispatch Section, Flight Planning, Maps and Charts Section and the Administration Section; assisting the Base Operations Chief in administrative duties of his office; utilization and control of space, equipment and supplies. Have ability to utilize computors for managerial functions. As early as 1962, excluding cost of equipment and buildings, was responsible for over $150,000 in supplies and expendible properties.

February 2, 1942 to September 8, 1958. Several Bases, USAF. During this period, began as an administrative clerk maintaining Flight Records and writing orders to become shift supervisor and then to become non-commissioned officer in charge. Progressed through a variety of managerial positions to become MSGT in present duty station. During these years, have always had to work with pilots, navigators, and staff officers in positions which demanded tact and diplomacy. Consider tact and diplomacy as well as my ability to motivate others to excel to be among my primary attributes.

HONORS

Although I have received several honors, the following one of greatest significance: The Air Force Commendation Medal with first oak leaf cluster for outstanding performance of both technical and administrative requirements "to the development of revised procedures which greatly improved the efficiency of staff actions in the Operations complex" and for "outstanding managerial skill and professionalism aided...in resolving countless problems associated with the problems involved in reporting the flying accomplishments of the wing." Have also been privileged to be president of the NCO Academy Graduates Association and of the Toastmaster's Club.

INTERESTS   Am highly interested in community oriented activities such as BPOE
             Elks, F&AM Masonic Lodge, Toastmasters; as well as in photography,
             golf, music, and furniture renovation. Enjoy being involved in
             activities such as Red Cross, Heart Fund drives and in orphanage
             and church work.

REFERENCES   References are available upon request.

Dr. Harold C. Grattan
2 Addoms Place South
Plattsburgh, New York 12901
518 563-6195 (Home)
518 564-3135 (Office)

Date of Birth: October 2, 1930
Marital Status: Wife, Ruth
    Stephen (10 yrs.), Kathy (6 yrs.)
Health: Very Good

EDUCATION:

1954-1957   University of Illinois, Urbana, Illinois. Received the B.S. with double majors in English and Speech.

1957-1959   University of Illinois, Urbana, Illinois. Received the Ed.M. in School Administration with minor in Communication.

1961-1964   University of Michigan, Ann Arbor, Mich. During these years plus the summers of 1960 through 1966, pursued the Ph.D. in Rhetoric and Public Address. Degree awarded December, 1966.

Since 1967, have attended institutes, short courses, and regularly audited courses.

TEACHING CAREER:

Sept. 1969   to Present: State University of New York College of Arts and Science, Plattsburgh, New York. Since initial appointment as Professor of Communication and Theatre Arts, have served as Chairman, Department of Communication and Theatre Arts (4 yrs.); and, as Coordinator of the General Studies Degree Programs since June, 1973. Requested to come to New York as Chairman of the Department of Com. and Theatre Arts which was on academic probation. In three years led the department from six members to seventeen (14 Ph.D's) and saw its enrollment increase to nearly 2000 per semester. In 1973, the department was recognized as one of the two strongest in the University and continues to earn the respect of the Faculty. In addition to administrative assignments, have taught two or more courses each semester at both the undergraduate and graduate levels. Currently, at the request of the administration, am coordinating, developing, and building the General Studies Programs. These programs have enjoyed significant growth and recognition. Also do extensive research and teaching within a contract with the Air Force.

Sept. 1966   to Aug. 1969: Central Michigan University, Mt. Pleasant, Mich. Served as Associate Professor of Speech and as Director of Forensics (included a major debate program). Specific duties included teaching at both undergraduate and graduate levels and directing graduate M.A. theses.

Sept. 1964   to Aug. 1966: Western Michigan University, Kalamazoo, Michigan. Instructor in Communication and Director of Forensics. Primarily business communication within School of Business.

Sept. 1961   to Aug. 1964: University of Michigan, Ann Arbor. Trueblood Scholar and Graduate Teaching Assist. Taught three courses per sem. plus summers due to previous teaching experience. Appointed Predoctoral Instructor three-fourths time teaching business and prof. speaking and directing debate in 1963. Co-taught a course with Prof. Gail Densmore in executive development each summer from 1962 through 1966 inclusive.

Sept. 1959   to June 1961: Lincoln-Way High School, New Lenox, Illinois. Teacher of English and Speech and Director of Forensics and Drama.

Sept. 1957   to June 1959: Beecher High School, Beecher, Ill. Teacher of English and Speech and Director of Forensics and Drama. During the summer of 1958, was Associate Director of a Ford Foundation Grant for Disadvantaged Children (in reading).

Dr. Harold C. Grattan—A highly experienced college educator/administrator.

ADMINISTRATIVE AND LEADERSHIP ROLES:

Sept. 1969 to present: State University College of Arts and Science, Plattsburgh, New York. Chairman, Department of Communication and Theatre Arts (1969 to Aug. 1973); Coordinator of General Studies and of Interdisciplinary Studies both since 1973; President of the local chapter of the AAUP (1971); Chairman, Faculty Senate 1972 to 1974; Secretary, Faculty Senate 1971; member of President's Shaping Committee (an advisory committee); member President's Executive Comm. without vote (1973); member of both the Instructional Resources and of the Library Advisory Committees; and an ex officio member of every Faculty Senate Standing Committee (1972-1974); Chairman, Faculty Affairs Comm. (1973-present); Chairman, Graduate Advisory Committee (current); member, President's Commission on Educational Priorities; served on College Budget Committee; plus others.

Special: Contract Administrator for a contract to provide 81 sections of a course entitled "Leadership and Communications for the E-7's, E-8's, and E-9's" allocated to twenty bases within the SAC Eighth Air Force. Duties include research and preparation of all course materials; selection and orientation of all instructional personnel from across the United States; and all budgetary aspects.

Sept. 1967 to Aug. 1969: Central Michigan University. Chairman, Public Address Area; Parliamentarian, Faculty Senate; President's representative to the Faculty Senate (1968-69); Chairman, Constitution Revision Committee; Chairman Faculty Research and Creative Endeavors Committee (awarded over $32,000 in local faculty awards each year); member of the Committee on Committees (elected at-large in 1968); Chairman, of both the Graduate and of the Undergraduate Scholarship Committees (involved over 150 scholarship awards); and a member of the University Curriculum Committee.

Sept. 1961 to Present: Have held offices in professional societies such as Executive Secretary for the Michigan Speech Assoc. (66-69); Parliamentarian of the Leadership Enclaves of the 66,000 member Michigan Education Assoc.; Parliamentarian of the New York State Reading Association; Parliamentarian of the Evangelical Lutherans in Mission national convention; member of several committees in Speech Communication Association of America, Michigan Speech Assoc., and New York Speech Assoc. Currently a past president of the local AAUP. Am a certified parliamentarian in the American Institute of Parliamentarians.

SCHOLARLY PUBLICATIONS AND CONVENTION PAPERS:

A Critical Analysis of Variations among Concepts of Persuasion and Conviction. Doctoral Dissertation, University of Michigan (December, 1966). Also read as a convention paper before the National Convention of the Speech Assoc. of America and appears in Convention Abstracts for 1969.

Speak With Confidence, a series of thirty-minute video modules for the beginning communication course at Plattsburgh. Prepared and produced three of the modules of thirty minutes each: "Choosing the Topic and Planning the Introduction"; "Planning the Body and the Conclusion"; and "Audience Analysis". All were funded and all are copyrighted by State University College, Plattsburgh.

"Future Directions of the Beginning Communications Course", paper read before the New York State Speech Association, March 1973.

"A Small School in Beecher, Illinois, Makes Big Strides", The Bulletin of the National Assoc. of Secondary School Principals, Vol. 43, No. 243 (Jan. 1959) in collaboration with Mr. John French and Dr. Edith Grotberg.

"A Doctrine of 'Equal Time' for Christian Educators", Lutheran Scholar, Vol. XXII, Nov. 4 (Oct. 1965).

"A Perspective on Changes in Pi Kappa Delta Debating", The Forensic, No. 1, (Oct. 1967), pp. 3-6.

"Valhalla Revisited", Michigan Speech Journal, Vol. IV, 1969.

"Improving Articulation Among United States Air Bases and Colleges", paper read before the Strategic Air Command's Education Officers Conference, Dallas, Texas, October 1973.

"Leadership and Communication for the 'Top Three' ", a paper read before a section of the AEA/NAPCAE National Convention at Dallas, Texas, October 1973.

"Leadership and Communication for the 'Top Three' ", a 21-page paper prepared for the Eighth Air Force and currently distributed to over 7,000 personnel.

2

PUBLIC ADDRESS AND CONFERENCE PRESENTATIONS:

Note: Since 1960, I have presented over four hundred speeches and conference presentations. A few samples follow:

"Developing Organizational and Individual Interest", a two hour presentation before nineteen Senior Citizens organizations (October 1975).

"The Process of Preparing Resumes and Letters of Application", all-day conference for over 600 students at current college (each year by request) and before other colleges, high schools and military groups.

"Understanding Parliamentary Procedure", a frequent topic before student and civic groups.

"A Time of Challenge", major address as honored speaker at the 22nd Annual National Prayer Breakfast at the Plattsburgh Air Force Base, February 1973.

"Time Honored Traditions vs. Change", major address as guest of honor at the "Dining Out" of the 380th Combat Support Group (SAC), Plattsburgh Air Force Base, 1974.

"Concepts of Management—Human Relations", Command and Staff College Seminar, Lockbourne Air Force Base, Ohio, 1974.

"Coaching the Comparative Advantages Case", Mich. Ed. Assoc. Regional Conf. in Saginaw (a six-hour workshop), 1969.

"The Use of Evidence and Reasoning—Case Construction", M.E.A. Regional Conference in Plymouth, Mich. 1964.

"The Evolution of the American Woman as a Public Speaker", Honors Colloquium at Central Michigan University, 1968.

"An Audience Centered Approach to Homiletics", and "Techniques of Audience Adaptation for Ministers", two papers read before the Saginaw Valley Assoc. of Lutheran Ministers in January 1970.

Workshop in "Leadership and Communication" for Management before Champlain Valley Management Association, N. Y. in 1974 and 1975.

COMMUNITY SERVICE:

United Fund (State Univ. Col. of Arts and Science-Plattsburgh Co-Chairman for 1973-74). Involved each year.

Council, Redeemer Lutheran Church (President 1970 to 1973).

Member of the Education Services Board of the Atlantic District of the Lutheran Church. Also elected delegate to the Atlantic District and to the National Conv., 1973 to present.

Conducted several seminars for the Clinton Correctional Officers and for the Plattsburgh Air Force Base.

Member of the Lions Club, the United States Power Squadron, and Cub Master for Cub Scouts.

HONORS:

Ilinois Veterans Scholarships, 1959; Trueblood Scholarship at the University of Michigan, 1961; University Research Grant at Central Michigan University in 1968; University Research Grant at State University College, Plattsburgh, 1970; Ford Foundation Grant co-recipient in 1957; currently, have personally received a total of $297,000 in contracts with the United States Eighth Air Force; member of Phi Delta Kappa; Pi Kappa Delta; Delta Sigma Rho; Lutheran Academy of Scholars; an honorary member of the Officers Open Mess at the 380th Combat Support Group at Plattsburgh Air Force Base; Univ. of Cincinnati Outstanding Debate Coach Award (twice: 1967-68); nominated for an "Outstanding Teacher Award" by Student Senate of Central Michigan University (1968); recipient of a banquet in my honor by over one hundred graduate students (1975); and received presidential merit increases in 1971 and 1974.

3

SUMMARY STATEMENT:

My philosophy is to do my best to meet the goals of the college, of the students, and of the faculty. We must build upon existing strengths, work to improve areas which might be weak, and have the courage to eliminate redundacies, to seek new directions and to encourage new concepts. I am fully committed to meaningful consultations of both faculty and students. I am committed to the "humane" aspect of the humanities and believe strongly in giving constructive criticism while preserving the dignity of the individual.

Trust is earned and an absolute requisite to successful leadership in today's colleges. In this respect you will find me fair but firm; one who carries out his responsibilities and one who believes in proper delegation; one who supports his administrators and yet expresses his differences of opinion as necessary. I am committed to strong teaching and research. Overall, I believe we can have strong teachers who are not prolific publishers; however, I do believe the best teaching is founded on solid research. Finally, I believe strongly in community service and in viable innovative programs.

Reference Books to U.S. Businesses and Corporations

To aid the reader to prepare a selected list of potential employers, with names and addresses, the following reference works are recommended as most helpful. From them one can easily compile a list of companies that offer opportunities within one's interests. In addition, one can learn much about the companies, their subsidiaries, products or services, and growth potential.

Since most of these sources are difficult to obtain on one's own, the reader is urged to consult with the Reference Librarian. The Reference Librarian will be able to tell you which ones are available in your local library. Some libraries may have other sources not listed here; or, possibly, they may maintain a Vertical File with information about local companies.

Allen's Personnel Directory of the Chemical Plants and Oil Refineries. Philadelphia: H. & D. Allen. Annual.

Angel, Juvenal L. *Directory of American Firms Operating in Foreign Countries.* 1955/56--. New York: World Trade Academy. Printed Irregularly.

Barron's Profiles of American Colleges. Benjamine Fine, Comp. (9th ed.) 1974. Woodbury, N.Y.: Barron's Educational Series, Inc.

The College Blue Book of Occupational Information. Max M. Russell, ed. (2nd ed., 1973). New York: Macmillan Publishing Company, Inc.

Directory of Corporate Affiliations of Major Corporations ("Who Owns Whom"). Skokie, Ill.: National Register Publishing Co. 1967-- An Annual with 3 supplements.

Directory of Shopping Centers in the United States and Canada. (1st ed., 1957/58--). Burlington, Ia.: National Research Bureau. Annual.

Dun & Bradstreet, Inc. Middle Market Directory. 1964--. New York. Annual.

————. *Million Dollar Directory.* 1959--. New York. Annual, with semiannual cumulated supplements.

These are companion volumes. The former lists about 31,000 businesses with net worth of $500,000 to $999,999; the latter about 33,000 businesses with net worth of $1 million or more. Each directory gives business name, state of incorporation, address, annual sales, and the number of employees and company officers and directors. Also lists officers, directors, alphabetically.

Dun & Bradstreet, Inc. *Dun & Bradstreet Reference Book of Corporate Managements.* 1967--. New York. Annual.

Industrial Research Laboratories of the United States. (1st ed.--, 1920--). Washington, D.C.: National Academy of Sciences, 1920-1960; New York: Bowker, 1965--. Irregularly.

The Thirteenth Edition (1970) provides information on over 5,000 non-governmental laboratories of over 3,000 organizations. Includes addresses, research staff and administration, and fields of research interest.

Insurance Almanac: Who, What, Where and When in Insurance; an Annual of Insurance Facts. 1912--. New York: Underwriter Printing and Publishing Co. Annual.

MacMillan Job Guide to American Corporations. 1967. New York: The MacMillan Company.

Moody's Industrial Manual: American and Foreign. 1964. New York: Moody's Investors Service.

New York Times Guide to College Selection. Ella Mazel, ed. Chicago: Quadrangle Books. Annual.

_____. *Guide to Continuing Education in America.* Prepared by the College Examination Board, Frances C. Thomson, ed. New York: Quadrangle Books. 1972.

Occupational Outlook Handbook. (Vols. 1949--). Washington, D.C.: U.S Bureau of Labor Statistics.

Sheldon's Retail, Department, Drygood, and Specialty Stores. 1884--. New York: Phelon-Sheldon & Marsar. Annual.

Standard and Poor's Corporation Records. New York: Standard and Poor's Corporation (a current, cumulative news of corporation descriptions).

_____. Industry Surveys. New York: McGraw-Hill, Inc. (looseleaf, updated monthly).

This is an extensive compilation of industrial surveys which provides current insights into trends and developments within corporations.

_____. *Register of Corporations, Directors and Executives.* New York: Standard and Poor's. Annual since 1928. 3 supplements a year.

The main section gives executive rosters and business telephone numbers of 33,000 companies in the U.S. and Canada. The section on individuals provides a brief biography for about 75,000 directors and executives.

Thomas' Register of American Manufacturers. 1906--. New York: Thomas Publishing Co. Annual.

An eleven volume work. Vols. 1-6 list products and services; Vol. 7 provides an alphabetical list of companies, their addresses, subsidiaries, products, and so forth; Vol. 8 gives an index to product classifications, trade names, and commercial organizations. Vol. 9-11, catalogs of companies.

25,000 Leading U.S. Corporations. 1970. New York: News Front. A computerized analysis of the 25,000 leading U.S. corporations.

Wiesenberger Services, Inc. Investment Companies. 1941--. New York. Annual.

Provides thorough and factual information on investment companies and their management.

OTHER SOURCES OF INFORMATION

The sources listed here are intended to provide the reader insights into the wealth of information available in newspapers and other periodicals. While these entries do represent some of the more widely known references, the applicant may find the information best suited to his needs in a local newspaper or in materials available at a Chamber of Commerce.

Barron's National Business and Financial Weekly. Boston.

Business Week.

"The Fortune Directory of the Largest Industrial Companies and Banks— Outside the U.S." *Fortune.* 89:202-35, September, 1973.

"The Fortune Directory of the 300 Largest Corporations Outside the U.S." *Fortune.* 92:155-62, August, 1975.

"Fortune's Directory of the 500 Largest Industrial Corporations." *Fortune.* 91:208-35, May, 1975.

"Fortune's Directory of the Largest Non-Industrial Companies." *Fortune.* 92:114-29, July, 1975.

"Fortune's Directory of the Second 500 Largest Industrial Corporations." *Fortune.* 91:120-48, June, 1975.

Harvard Business Review.

Occupational Outlook Quarterly. U.S. Government Printing Office.1957 to present.

New York Times.

"200 Leading Performers." *Dun's Review.* 106:54-57, December, 1975.

Wall Street Journal.

"Where To Find the Company." *Forbes.* 117:43-44+, January 1, 1976.

Index

OTHER SELF-HELP/CAREER AIDS
AVAILABLE FROM

Prentice Hall Press

Look for them wherever books are sold, or use the
handy order blank below for home delivery.

Quanity	Title	Order #	Price
_____	THE ART OF TALKING SO THAT PEOPLE WILL LISTEN Swets	04783-7	$5.95
_____	INTERVIEWING THE INTERVIEWER Merman/McLaughlin	64512-6	$9.95
_____	HOW TO WIN IN A JOB INTERVIEW Robertson	43951-3	$6.95
_____	THE LAST WORD ON THE GENTLE ART OF VERBAL SELF-DEFENSE Elgin	52406-6	$9.95
_____	MAKING MORE MONEY 55 Special Job-Hunting Strategies for Retirees Mitchell	41790-7	$7.95
_____	MORE ON THE GENTLE ART OF VERBAL SELF-DEFENSE Elgin	60112-0	$7.95
_____	THE PROFESSIONAL RESUME & JOB SEARCH GUIDE Dickhut	72570-5	$8.95
_____	SELLING YOURSELF The Way to a Better Job Jeffers	80607-5	$6.95
_____	WRITING A JOB-WINNING RESUME McLaughlin/Merman	97022-8	$6.95

Prices subject to change without notice

☐ Please charge my ☐ MasterCard ☐ Visa

Credit Card # _____ Exp. date _____

Signature _____

☐ Enclosed is my check or money order.
   *Publisher pays postage and handling charges
    for prepaid and charge card orders.

☐ Bill me.

Name _____ Apt. # _____

Address _____

City/State _____ Zip _____

MERCHANDISE TOTAL		
ADD:	SALES TAX FOR YOUR STATE	
	*12% POSTAGE AND HANDLING	
TOTAL: CHECK ENCLOSED		

PLEASE ALLOW FOUR WEEKS FOR DELIVERY

Send your order to:
PH Mail Order Billing
Route 59 at Brook Hill Drive
West Nyack, NY 10994

Phone (201) 767-5937 for
any additional ordering
information.